The
(Almost)
No Fat
COOKBOOK

Everyday Vegetarian Recipes

Bryanna Clark Grogan

Book Publishing Company • Summertown, Tennessee

© 1994 Bryanna Clark Grogan

Cover by Richard Curtis
Interior design by Barbara McNew

Printed in the United States by Book Publishing Company
PO Box 99
Summertown, TN 38483

Grogan, Bryanna Clark, 1948-
       The almost no fat cookbook : everyday vegetarian recipes / by Bryanna Clark
       Grogan.
                        p.   cm.
                Includes index.
                ISBN 0-913990-12-4
                1. Vegetarian cookery, 2. Vegetarianism   I. Title.
       TX837.G676 1994
       641.5'636--dc20   94-9594
                                                                      CIP

Dedication

This book is for Brian.

Acknowledgments

Many thanks to Drs. Dean Ornish, Neal Barnard, Julian Whitaker, and John McDougall for leading the way. Also, thanks to John Robbins and Dr. Michael Klaper of EarthSave, the *Laurel's Kitchen* gang, and The Farm people for inspiring millions to the vegetarian way of life, and to Frances Moore Lappé for her pioneering work.

Contents

Author's Notes 4

Introduction 6

The Basics 21

Appetizers, Snacks & Sandwiches 51

Breakfast & Breads 67

Soups, Salads & Dressings.................... 85

Oven-Baked Entrees 103

Top-of-the Stove Entrees 120

Side Dishes 133

Desserts 144

Glossary 178

Cooking Charts 186

Index.. 188

Our relationship with food is connected to some of our deepest feelings and earliest memories. For this reason, as well as cultural conditioning, changing our eating patterns may be one of the most difficult and revolutionary shifts of habit and consciousness in our lives. We must have powerful motivation for doing so.

For a growing number of people, the motivation for dietary change is a sustainable future—for the planet, and thus for ourselves. For many others, the motivation may be to win a battle against heart disease, cancer, diabetes, and the like. Still others want to lose weight and keep it off after years of guilt-inducing and energy-draining diets.

Powerful motivation may get us going in the right dietary direction, but it's going to be our daily food that keeps us on course. It doesn't matter how much food we eat if it doesn't taste good.

And what tastes good to us, especially in times of stress and change, is usually something familiar. The recipes in this book are designed to look and taste familiar even as they present a new style of cooking and eating, and what may seem to be some very unfamiliar ingredients (such as soy sauce, nutritional yeast flakes, and tofu). Despite some unorthodox ingredients, there are no recipes more exotic here than lasagne and chile.

You or a loved one are making some very big changes in a very important aspect of life: diet. If you make these changes as painlessly as possible, they will become the norm. Give yourself time to learn—six months from now steam-frying instead of sautéing in butter or oil will seem second-nature to you. Shopping and menu-planning will no longer take much effort as all of these "new" foods will be old friends. You'll have a repertoire of favorite dishes and the cooking know-how to explore other cuisines and more complicated techniques.

Fat paranoia may seem an odd thing to address in an almost fat-free cookbook, but I have a concern about the

American tendency to go to extremes, especially when it comes to food and diet. I don't want people to get so carried away with avoiding fats that they take the joy out of life or, even worse, start a new type of eating disorder. We must have a little fat in our diets, in the form of essential fatty acids, in order to absorb fat-soluble nutrients (vitamins A, D, E, and K) and to keep our skin and hair smooth and shiny. Fat is also important (especially for children) for cell growth.

Obviously, I embrace a very low-fat, vegetarian (vegan if possible) diet as the easiest and best way to lose weight and keep it off, to prevent cancer, to prevent or reverse heart disease, and to live, if not longer, then in better health and vitality. I wrote this book in order to smooth the way for others who would like to benefit from this life-style as much as I have.

When you are used to this new style of cooking and have found or devised delicious recipes, it's not a deprivation to eat this way. Cooking and eating are so important to me that I wouldn't be able to stay nearly fat-free if it wasn't enjoyable.

Sometimes I can't control what I am eating or how it is cooked—at parties, dinners with friends, meals in restaurants, or on feast days. I go ahead and eat moderately of foods containing nuts, olives, avocado, oil and (even some fried things and sweets) without guilt and with enjoyment. And do you know what? I don't gain weight overnight (even on a 2-week holiday trip). I know from experience that I can't eat like this all the time, but I don't want to anymore.

If you have a severe health problem, you will probably have to be more strict than I am on festive occasions. And if you eat out often (I do very seldom), you'll have to learn some "tricks of the trade" (see pgs. 14-16). But in either case, there's no need to become a "diet bore" or a "fat fanatic": let your slim figure, obvious good health, and vitality be natural advertisements for your new style of eating.

To your good health and good appetite!
Bryanna Clark Grogan

Introduction

We all have our obsessions. Some people are baseball fanatics, others collect spoons or thimbles. I cook. And think about what to cook. And eat, of course—that's the best part!

I used to cook and eat nearly everything, but about six years ago I realized I didn't really want to eat meat anymore. That was an interesting challenge for me, and I got really excited about vegetarian food and its possibilities. It didn't take long before I decided to become a vegan—that is, do away with eggs and dairy products in my diet, as well as meat products, fish, and poultry. I've taken great delight in creating an interesting and varied vegan cuisine that my non-vegetarian family and friends can also enjoy—and they do!

But it seems that I continue to challenge myself in the cooking department. The work of Dr. Dean Ornish (see pg. 185) convinced me that a very low-fat diet would control a possible inherited cholesterol problem *and* keep my middle-aged waistline (and my husband's too—not to mention *his* cholesterol) from expanding. I was already trying to keep our fat level low and using only cold-pressed olive and canola oils. But it seemed that oil sneaked into everything, and I couldn't resist throwing in a few more olives, or nuts . . . .

Now I wish that it hadn't taken me so long to try Dr. Ornish's no-added-fat plan. I decided to try it for a month, and after the month was over, I realized that we'd lost weight without having to worry about portions or calories or fat grams, *and* we were really enjoying the food.

This way of cooking and eating isn't about Spartanism or deprivation—no way! You don't need to cook with fat of any kind to appreciate the sensuous nature of chopping and slicing red peppers and green broccoli and purple eggplants, kneading and rolling some *Sweet Yeast Bread Dough*, pg. 81, and steam-frying aromatic onions, garlic, chiles, and herbs.

If you're skeptical, all I can say is, "Try the recipes!" Once you get used to steam-frying instead of sautéing, baking instead of deep-frying, using deep-flavored, dried mushrooms instead of olives, and browned flour instead of brown roux, you'll truly wonder (as I did) why it took you so long to try cooking this way. And instead of concentrating on what you can't have anymore (or what you choose not to have), dwell on all the wonderful foods that you have at your disposal—crisp, colorful vegetables, juicy, sweet fruits, aromatic herbs, spices, onions, and garlic, the whole gamut of grains and beans, homey and comforting potatoes, breads, and pastas (or elegant and trendy, depending on your mood). Let's face it, most people on the standard, American, meat-based diet eat pretty boring stuff. You can eat boring stuff on this type of diet too, but there's no need.

We all have our own style of cooking and eating. I like to think of my own style as eclectic—drawing from many different sources. You'll find easy, homey recipes here, using such conveniences as garlic granules and canned tomato paste. You'll also find some recipes with unusual ingredients such as nutritional yeast flakes and textured vegetable protein. They are used so that the resulting flavors and textures will be familiar and comforting.

If there is a shortcut or a substitute that still results in good eating, I'll let you know. I have a family and a job, and I know that it's just not possible to cook the way a restaurant chef does very often.

As Dr. Dean Ornish says, it's often easier to make big changes in your life than little ones. When you aren't using oils and other added fats at all, there's no worrying about measuring and draining and counting fat grams. When you aren't eating meat, you don't have to weigh portions and cut off fat and discard the skin. When you aren't eating dairy products and eggs, you won't have to read labels for fat content and throw yolks down the drain. But you *will* be able to eat your fill of delicious food and leave the table satisfied. Talk about having your cake and eating it too!

How Much Fat Is Too Much?

You're apt to see the quantity of fat in a food measured as a *percentage of calories* in that food. This is because nutritionists are recommending what proportion of calories in our diet should come from fat. Standard recommendations for good health are currently 30% of calories from fat; recent reports from researchers recommend much lower levels— around 10% to 15%—to achieve weight loss and protect against heart disease and cancer.

After eating a low-fat diet for a while, you probably won't need to count fat grams at all, but in the beginning it might help you to see how much fat you are eating (or how little). A moderately active man weighing about 150 lbs. can eat about 25 grams of fat a day to stay in the 10% calories from fat range; a moderately active woman weighing 130 lbs. can eat 20 grams daily. If you are less active, eat a couple of grams less; if you are more active, you can eat a few more. If your ideal weight is more or less than this, adjust your fat intake accordingly.

It's not too difficult to calculate the percentage of calories from fat that you eat each day. A gram of fat will provide 9 calories when consumed. If over a day's time you've eaten 20 grams of fat and 1800 calories, you can calculate the percentage of calories from fat like this:

20 grams fat x 9 calories per gram = 180 calories from fat

180 calories from fat/1800 total calories = 10% of calories from fat

This is a fairly easy example to calculate. When the numbers get more complicated, (72 grams of fat and 2330 calories, for example), round up a little and get a close approximation (multiply fat grams by 10 instead of 9, so that 72 grams x 10 = 720 calories; 720 calories is a little less than ⅓ of 2330, so the percentage is around 30%).

Although considering the percentage of fat in your total diet can be useful, looking at individual foods or recipes this way can be misleading. A food can be low in fat, but be so low in calories as well that the *percentage* of fat to calories can look deceivingly high (as with regular tofu, which has only 82 calories in a 4 oz. serving, but half those calories come from fat). A calorie-dense food, such as one high in sugar, might have a lower *percentage* of calories from fat, but actually contain more fat per serving. If you planned on eating quite a bit of just one food, you might want to look at the percentage of calories from fat in that one food, but we rarely eat like this. The best way to keep your fat level down to about 10% of total calories is to follow the nutrition guide on pg. 12, don't use added oils and fats, eat only plant foods, and keep high-fat plant foods to a bare minimum.

Tofu deserves some additional mention because so much has been written about its high percentage of fat. As I demonstrated in the previous paragraph, 50% of the calories in regular tofu come from fat. But the total amount of calories in tofu are very low, much lower than equivalent amounts of avocado, nuts, etc., and much lower than eggs, oil, and solid cooking fats. When I use 8 ounces of regular tofu in my basic muffin recipe for 12 muffins, each muffin has less than 1 gram of fat (and reduced-fat tofu lowers it even more). A traditional, "low-fat" muffin recipe with 1 large egg and ¼ cup of oil (not counting any nuts that might be added) would contain about 58 grams of fat or close to 5 grams per muffin.

The truth is that soy foods are good for us. Study after study confirms that soy foods of all kinds can significantly lower blood cholesterol, are an excellent source of iron in the diet, and may have a major role in cancer prevention.

Tofu is probably the most versatile soy food since it can be used not only as meat substitute, but also as a replacement for high-fat dairy products and eggs. Also, tofu and soymilk provide a natural way to ingest unprocessed essential fatty acids without the need for expensive oil supplements. As long as fruits, vegetables, whole grains, and legumes make up the majority of your diet (and nuts, oils, seeds, olives, and avocados are only occasional treats), tofu, soymilk, and other soy foods can play important supporting roles.

If you are still concerned about the fat in tofu and soy foods, investigate the lower-fat soy products that are coming into the market: reduced-fat soymilk, tofu, and silken tofu. I have used reduced-fat tofu throughout the book to demonstrate how you can use it to cut back on fat even more than with regular tofu. If you cannot find the reduced-fat products in your area, you may substitute the full-fat products without affecting the outcome of the recipes. There are many low-fat vegetarian hot dogs and burgers on the market too, and textured vegetable protein is naturally almost fat-free (see pg. 25).

A Word About Nutrition

A full discussion of nutrition is beyond the scope of this book. I urge you to consult the books listed in the bibliography so that you will have solid nutritional information to work with.

Here are a few things to keep in mind:

✔ Anyone who eats enough calories to maintain their body weight and energy level is getting enough protein (perhaps more than enough).

✔ As long as you eat a varied diet, you don't need to worry about combining proteins (eating beans and grains at the same meal, etc.)

✔ All known nutrients (with the possible exceptions of vitamin B₁₂ and vitamin D) are adequately supplied by a *varied* diet of any whole, vegetarian foods which supply you enough calories for good health. You can meet your requirement for vitamin B₁₂ by taking 25 mcg. each week in pill form, or eating nutritional yeast flakes that have B₁₂ added. If you expose your face and arms to the sun (even on a cloudy day) for 10 to 15 minutes a day, your body will naturally produce enough vitamin D. I recommend that you take some vitamin D from a vegetable source during the winter if you live in a northern climate or are nursing or pregnant.

✔ Over-consumption of protein, *not* under-consumption of calcium, may be an important factor contributing to osteoporosis. World health statistics show that the disease is most common in countries where dairy products are consumed in large quantities.

Rich vegetarian sources of calcium are kale, dried legumes, sesame meal, blackstrap molasses, green leafy vegetables, carob, soy flour, tofu made with calcium salts (most commercial tofu is these days), dried fruit, nutritional yeast, corn tortillas and masa harina, acorn squash, and sea vegetables. If you are still concerned about calcium, take calcium carbonate, the cheapest, most concentrated, and easily-absorbed form. Get plenty of exercise, avoid alcohol and tobacco, and reduce your consumption of caffeine and soft drinks.

✔ You do not need to eat red meat for iron. Some excellent vegetarian sources of iron are sea vegetables, prunes and other dried fruits, prune juice, nutritional yeast, blackstrap molasses, beans, soy foods, whole grains, potatoes, sesame meal, and fresh peas. Dairy products lack iron and can block iron absorption. Your iron absorption is increased by eating plenty of foods rich in vitamin C, such as fruits and vegetables, not drinking caffeinated beverages (including tea) with meals, and cooking in cast iron pots. The Chinese have excellent iron levels despite high levels of fiber and low levels of red meat in their diet.

Here is a basic eating guideline that you can divide up into meals in whatever way is comfortable for you:

Every day have at least:

4 servings of whole grains (1 slice bread or ½ cup cooked grain or pasta)

and

3 servings of vegetables (¾ cup cooked greens or 1 cup other vegetable). Include at least one dark green or orange vegetable or ½ cup dried legumes, cooked.

Fill out your calorie, vitamin, and mineral needs with a variety of whole foods, including:

fruit

high-carbohydrate vegetables (artichokes, potatoes, sweet potatoes, beets, carrots, parsnips, squash, turnips, peas, corn, etc.)

low-calorie vegetables (tomatoes, green beans, cauliflower, cucumber, eggplants, mushrooms, lettuce, peppers, etc.)

more whole grains, dried legumes, and dark green and orange vegetables

soy foods and seitan (wheat gluten)

nutritional yeast

sea vegetables (kelp, kombu, wakame, arame, etc.)

If you are pregnant, nursing, ill, or under stress, you will need to include more concentrated proteins (tofu, tempeh, textured vegetable protein, other soy foods and seitan). If you are expending large amounts of energy, you will need more grains, fruits, and high-carbohydrate vegetables.

Eat a variety of whole foods in as close to their natural state as possible.

Children, Fat, and Vegetarian Diets

According to a joint study from the Center for Disease Control and The Farm (a vegetarian community), children raised on a strict vegetarian (vegan) diet can grow normally, provided that they eat a well-rounded diet with plenty of protein from soy products and legumes. Ideally, they should be breast-fed for at least a year, adding solids after six months or so. (Check the bibliography on pg. 185 for several helpful books for parents on vegetarian nutrition for children.)

It is as difficult to cover a complete discussion of vegetarian nutrition for children as it would be for adults, but I would just like to warn parents that children and adults have different dietary needs. While low-protein and high-fiber diets might be good for adults, a child who fills up on too much fiber may not be able to eat enough protein and obtain enough calories for proper growth. So feed your child the same things that you eat, but unless the child is very obese, add liberal amounts of nut and seed butters, tahini, hummus, pureed beans, avocado, and tofu. Keep nuts and dried fruits around for munching (watch small children with these, as they can choke on large pieces), and add molasses, wheat germ, and nutritional yeast to foods for extra calories and nutrients. Offer soymilk and tofu-fruit shakes, puddings, and frozen desserts. Pasta is a favorite. Go easy on fruit juice; it's filling and can dampen young appetites. Use soda water with fruit concentrates instead of soft drinks for special occasions.

Teens, provided they are not overweight, should continue to eat as outlined above, and they may eat astonishing amounts! Even overweight teens need about 20% of calories from fat and generous amounts of vegetarian foods in order to get the necessary amounts of protein, vitamins, and minerals required. The best way for overweight teens to supplement the adult diet is to eat plenty of soy products, which are high in protein, iron, and calcium (especially commercially prepared tofu, most of which is made with calcium salts). These foods will also provide extra fat in a natural, unprocessed form. Offer plenty of fresh fruit too.

Eating Out

If you dine out only occasionally, splurging on high-fat foods in a restaurant or at a party won't hurt once in a while. However, if you eat out often and/or you are on a low-fat diet for health reasons, you will have to be more careful. Assess your habits and see if it's not possible to eat at home more often. If that's not possible, here are some tips:

If you are flying, have your travel agent order low-fat, vegan meals well ahead of time. A fruit plate is also a good alternative. In either case, check with your airline about a day before your flight to make sure your request has been received. Bring a nutritious alternative snack to replace airline peanuts and chips.

If you are going to a party, speak with your host or hostess privately about your needs, and offer to bring some food that you can eat and others will also enjoy.

If you travel often, keep a supply of fat-free salad dressing in your car or briefcase. It can be a lifesaver if your only option is a salad, baked potato, or vegetable plate, but the sauces and salad dressings served with them are all high in fat. (Ask that your dish be served without the sauce or dressing.) Two baked potatoes and a large salad with fat-free dressing make a filling meal—try a fruit salad for dessert.

If you're eating at a restaurant, ask your waiter or waitress about what dishes on their menu are low-fat or fat-free. If they're unsure, ask if they can get a suggestion from the chef.

If you eat at the same restaurant(s) frequently, ask the waiters or chefs about putting together something that's within their scope, but just might not be on the menu.

Here are some specific ideas for different ethnic restaurants:

Chinese restaurants: Ask that chicken broth not be used. Ask that stir-fries be done in water, vegetable broth, or "dry-fried" (over high heat only). Good menu choices are steamed vegetarian dumplings, steamed rice (especially brown), steamed or stir-fried greens with tofu (bean curd) or gluten (ask that these not be fried first), steamed or braised vegetables, Buddha's Delight (mixed vegetables), vegetable soup without eggs or fried noodles. CHINESE

Indian restaurants: Ask that no ghee (clarified butter) be added to your food. Avoid rich desserts and fried foods, such as samosas and pakoras. Good menu choices are plain rice, dahl, and breads like naan or chapatis (all without ghee), dhoklas or idlis (steamed bean and rice cakes), chutneys and salads (no coconut), bean and vegetable dishes with no ghee or panir (cheese) added, roasted popadam (crisp legume wafers, not fried), and fresh fruit. INDIAN

French restaurants: Ask that no dressing, sauces, oil, or butter be added to the food. Good menu choices are French bread, vegetable side dishes and salads (with lemon juice or a lemon wedge on the side), and fresh fruit or sorbet. FRENCH

Italian restaurants: Avoid fresh pasta—it contains eggs. Ask that no butter, cheese, or oil be added. Good menu choices are vegetarian pizza without cheese, eggless potato gnocchi, pasta or vegetable-stuffed ravioli with vegetarian marinara (tomato) sauce, salad without dressing (ask for balsamic vinegar or a lemon wedge on the side), pasta e fagioli (pasta with beans), meatless minestrone soup, plain Italian bread, steamed vegetables, and fresh fruits or fruit ices and sorbets. ITALIAN

Mexican restaurants: Ask that no lard be used and that guacamole, avocado, sour cream, and cheese be served on the side (or not at all). Good menu choices are salsa with baked tortilla chips, beans without lard, salads with lemon juice, MEXICAN rice dishes without meat, lard, or cheese, bean burritos with rice and no cheese, baked or "dry-fried" quesadillas with beans or vegetables and no cheese, vegetable fajitas, and fresh fruits or fruit drinks.

GREEK

Greek or Middle Eastern restaurants: There are many vegan and vegetarian dishes available but most of them are prepared with lots of olive oil: Greek salad, hummus, stuffed grape leaves without meat, spanikopita, zucchini fritters, tabbouleh, etc. Eat in moderation, eat lots of vegetables, ask that no oil be added if possible, and fill up on plain pita bread.

VEGETARIAN

Vegetarian, natural foods, or health food restaurants: Check that foods are not laden with cheese and other dairy products, butter, oil, avocado, nuts, and seeds. Good menu choices are salads with lemon juice, vinegar, or your own dressing, whole grains and breads, vegetable dishes, fresh fruits, and fruit or tofu-fruit shakes.

Ingredients For a Low-Fat, Vegetarian Diet

Stocking up on ingredients for the recipes in this book may require a change in your usual shopping list. You won't have to buy oil anymore, except for greasing pans. And you can save the money you used to spend on eggs, dairy products, margarine, vegetable shortening, meat, fish, poultry, and any other product made from animals (lard, gelatin). You also won't need nuts, olives, avocados, coconut products, or seeds—except for a sprinkling of poppy or sesame seeds on the top of breads, and the occasional addition of some ground roasted sesame seeds (*Sesame Meal*, pg. 47), where the specific flavor of sesame would be missed. (I used to use roasted sesame oil and tahini for this purpose, but ground whole sesame seeds provide just as much flavor with far less fat and more fiber.)

Just about everything else there is to eat is raw material for almost no-fat cooking. Of course, you'll have to be cautious with packaged foods. Use breads, cereals, and crackers without added fats, or make your own. There are many fat-free products on the market today, but be sure they aren't loaded with sugar, salt, and artificial ingredients before you buy them. You'll want to nourish yourself with real food, not fool your taste buds with fat-free junk food. Use commercial products such as baked tortilla chips, fruit sorbets, fat-reduced soy, rice, or almond beverages, rye crisp crackers, and fat-free, whole grain cereals.

I do use salt, sugar, honey, and alcohol in my cooking. *Salt can be reduced* to your taste or replaced with salt substitutes and herbal blends, but remember that only a small percentage of the population needs to cut salt drastically out of the diet. The best way to cut down on salt is to do away with commercially processed foods (including cheese), which account for over 75% of the salt in the American diet. To further reduce salt, choose low-sodium soy sauce, sometimes referred to as "lite" soy sauce.

Sugar is a controversial subject. Some patients with heart disease (especially those with high triglycerides) are advised not to touch it; others are allowed it in moderation. There are alternatives, but nothing that suits everyone. If you prefer not to use honey, see pg. 146. All cane sugar *except* turbinado sugar is bleached with bone char made from beef bones (molasses is extracted before this process). If you are a vegetarian for ethical reasons, you can substitute beet sugar, or granulated sugar cane juice. See pg. 145 for more information. Please refer to the short discussion of sweeteners at the beginning of Chapter 8.

Even though most of the *alcohol* used in these recipes will evaporate during cooking, you may want to use a good, non-alcoholic (or reduced alcohol) wine or beer. Dry sherry may be replaced with a mixture of non-alcoholic, dry white wine and a little bit of frozen apple juice concentrate, or a fairly sweet, non-alcoholic white wine. Strong liquors such as rum or brandy can be replaced by juice or other liquid with a dash of the appropriate flavor extract added.

I use soy products in place of dairy products. Not only do they provide similar tastes and textures, they provide essential fatty acids in their natural form.

If you cannot use soy products, you can replace soymilk with commercial or *Plain Rice Milk* (see pg. 40). Some brands of commercial almond milk are also an option; despite being made from almonds, this product is quite low in fat. There are even potato-based milk beverages on the market. Tofu is difficult to replace; blended, cooked rice, millet, barley, and oatmeal can sometimes be used for creamy mixtures (soups, puddings, shakes, etc.). Seitan, a wheat-based product, can be used instead of frozen tofu or textured vegetable protein.

When a recipe calls for just "soymilk," it is because the amount of naturally occurring oil in regular, full-strength soymilk (either commercial or homemade) gives the best results. *If I call for "reduced-fat soymilk" or other non-dairy milk,* it means that you can use commercial or homemade, reduced-fat soymilk, *Tofu Milk*, pg. 39, or any of the alternate beverages mentioned in the earlier paragraph with equal

HOMEMADE,
REDUCED-FAT
SOYMILK

results. To make a *homemade, reduced-fat soymilk* you may dilute one quart (4 cups) of commercial or homemade, full-strength soymilk with 1½ cups water and get the same results.

Caffeine is a highly-addictive substance that affects insulin balance, so I recommend the use of Swiss, water-decaffeinated, organic coffee and water-decaffeinated tea, if you don't want to give up these beverages altogether. Do not use chemically-decaffeinated products (it must say "Swiss water-decaffeinated" to be sure that it is the real thing).

I don't recommend the use of artificial sweeteners or fats. Studies have shown that people who use them don't lose weight any more easily than people who don't use them. Artificial sweeteners and the new artificial fats, such as Olestra® and Simplesse® just keep your taste buds clamoring for more sweet, greasy foods. And the jury is not in yet on whether or not these foods may be harmful.

In some baking recipes, a low-gluten flour, such as *oat flour*, is required. You can use rice, millet, barley or other low-gluten flours if you prefer, but oats are common in most households and can easily and inexpensively be made into flour in your blender. Simply process rolled or quick oatmeal in your *dry* blender until it is the consistency of flour. Store the flour in a tightly-covered container in your freezer.

If you cannot afford to buy a set of non-stick pans (perhaps you can acquire one at a time as you replace old pans), oil your pans lightly with either *Non-stick Cooking Blend*, pg. 48, or canola, olive, or sesame oil. I keep these oils in small squirt bottles. Each full squirt equals ¼ tsp. of oil, and you rarely need more than two squirts. I spread the oil with my fingertips. *I do not use commercial, non-stick spray products* because they are expensive, I don't like the way they taste or smell, and I'm not sure that they are environmentally safe. In any case, the containers are not reusable and are difficult, if not impossible, to recycle.

If you are not familiar with some of the ingredients in this book, consult the glossary on pgs. 178-84. This glossary also contains information tofu, pasta, rice, agar, why I use cornstarch instead of arrowroot powder, and lots more, so give it a quick perusal before trying the recipes.

Steam-frying

One term that you will see over and over in my recipes is "steam-fry." What it means is simply stir-frying or sautéing without fat.

Use a heavy skillet (cast iron or stainless steel with an aluminum core or bottom), non-stick or lightly greased with about ½ tsp. of oil brushed on with your fingertips, or a well-seasoned wok, lightly greased.

Heat the pan over high heat, add your chopped vegetables and one or two tablespoons of liquid, depending on how many vegetables you are cooking. You can use water, broth, or wine for the liquid—keep a small measuring cup with a spout handy by the stove to add liquid as you cook. Cook over high heat until the liquid starts to evaporate, stirring with a spatula or wooden spoon. Keep doing this until the vegetables are done to your liking, adding *just enough* liquid to keep the vegetables from sticking to the bottom of the pan—you don't want to stew them!

You can brown onions perfectly with this method. As soon as the sugar from the onions starts to brown on the bottom and edges of the pan, add a little liquid and scrape the caramelized sugar, mixing it into the liquids and around into the cooking onions. Keep doing this until the onions are soft and brown, being careful not to scorch them.

> If you cannot find reduced-fat regular tofu, silken tofu, or soymilk in your area, you can use full-fat products in any of these recipes without affecting the outcome; just be aware that the fat content per serving will go up slightly.

Chapter 1

The Basics

You'll be referring to this chapter often, because it contains recipes that are used within other recipes—things like *Tofu Sour Cream* and *Seasoned Flour*. It will also provide recipes for some things which are available commercially (like rice milk and tofu cream cheese), but which may not be available in your area or may be too expensive to buy regularly.

You'll need a blender for many of these recipes, but it doesn't have to be a fancy, expensive one. I would also recommend buying a food processor (again, it doesn't need to be an expensive one unless you plan to use it for bread dough). It works better than a blender for chopping and for thick mixtures such as bean dips. I use mine several times a day, and there are many things that I just wouldn't make if I didn't own one. Otherwise, you need no special equipment.

I have not included recipes for time-consuming items such as homemade tofu and soymilk, because the average person is not going to make them on a regular basis. If you have trouble obtaining them in your town (be sure to check natural food stores, ethnic markets, and large supermarkets), check the publications on pg. 185 for manufacturers of the items you're looking for, and ask your store manager to order what you need. Tofu and soymilk are available in vacuum packs and tetra-packs that last weeks or months. Dry beans, grains, packaged egg replacer, nutritional yeast, broth powders, and dry textured vegetable protein all store easily for long periods of time. Your local market should have no objection to ordering these for you, especially if you or a group of friends buy in bulk (and this way you may get a special price).

Oven-Fried "Breast of Tofu"

Makes 16 slices

This is a staple in my house. I call it "breast of tofu," because it takes the place of chicken breast in sandwiches, stir-fries, salads, and many other dishes. I make the stir-fry variation up in quantity, bake it, and freeze it for future use (with waxed paper between the layers for easy removal).

Prepare *Breast of Tofu Marinade* by combining in a 2-quart bowl:

> 1½ cups water
> ¼ cup soy sauce
> 3 Tbsp. nutritional yeast flakes
> 2 tsp. crumbled sage leaves,
>   or 1 tsp. powdered sage
> ½ tsp. dried rosemary
> ½ tsp. dried thyme
> ½ tsp. onion powder

Instead of all or some of the traditional "poultry seasonings" (thyme, sage, rosemary, etc.), use cumin, coriander, basil, oregano, or whatever herbs are suitable for the dish you are making. For spicy Breast of Tofu, add as much Louisiana-style hot sauce to the marinade as you like.

Cut into ½-inch thick slices:

> **2 lbs. reduced-fat, firm or medium-firm regular tofu**

Marinate the tofu slices for as little as a few hours or as long as a few days (in the refrigerator). Turn the slices or spoon over the marinade from time to time, or store in a tightly lidded container, and shake.

To cook, preheat the oven to 400°F, and coat the tofu slices in:

> **1 cup Seasoned Flour, pg. 49**

Lay the slices in single layers, not touching, on two lightly greased, dark-colored cookie sheets (the tofu won't brown properly on shiny aluminum sheets). Bake until the bottoms are golden, about 15 minutes. Turn the pieces over and bake until the other sides are golden, about 15 minutes more. Use immediately or cool on racks and refrigerate.

The slices will keep well wrapped in the refrigerator for several days. Cold Breast of Tofu slices can be used as a sandwich "meat." Try them diced and mixed with celery and *Tofu Mayonnaise*, pg. 36, for an excellent sandwich filling or hearty salad to serve on lettuce leaves. Serve hot slices topped with any sauce suitable for chicken or veal. Use in your favorite casseroles, or slivered in a chef's salad instead of chicken.

Per slice: Calories: 74, Protein: 7 gm., Carbohydrates: 7 gm. Fat: 1 gm.

Stir-Fry "Chicken" Slivers

VARIATIONS

Cook as above, but do not coat in Seasoned Flour first. These can be frozen for up to 3 months. (For easy removal, freeze with pieces of waxed paper between the slices.) You can cut the frozen slices into slivers and add them to stir-fries or casseroles without having to brown them in the pan first— very convenient and tastier than using plain tofu. See also the *Smoky Baked Tofu* recipe on the next page.

Breaded "Breast of Tofu"

Dip the marinated tofu slices in **1 cup soymilk** which has been soured in **1 Tbsp. lemon juice**. Then dip in *Seasoned Coating Mix*, pg. 50, and oven bake as above. This is good hot or cold with ketchup, chili sauce, or *Tartar Sauce*, pg. 36.

If you don't have any Seasoned Coating mix, you can dip the slices first in plain flour, then in the soured soymilk, then in *Seasoned Flour*, pg. 49, and oven bake as usual.

VARIATION

Smoky Baked Tofu

Make up this easy recipe in quantity, and freeze some of it for future use in sandwiches, casseroles, enchiladas, etc.

For 2 pounds of firm regular tofu, make up a marinade of **1½ cups water, ¼ cup soy sauce, and 1 tsp. liquid smoke.** Cut the tofu into ½" thick slices, and marinate in the above mixture for several hours or several days in the refrigerator. To cook, lay the slices in single layers, not touching, on lightly greased, dark-colored cookie sheets. Bake at 400°F until the bottoms are golden. Turn the pieces over and bake until the other side is golden. Eat immediately or cool. Store in rigid plastic containers in the refrigerator for up to a week, or freeze for up to three months. (For easy removal, freeze with pieces of waxed paper between the slices.)

Bright Idea . . .

Marinated Tofu Cubes

These have always been well-liked by novice tofu-users in my workshops. They make a great, low-fat alternative to feta cheese, and the drained cubes can be crumbled in salads or on pizza.

Cut firm (not pressed) tofu into small cubes, and cover them in a bowl or jar with *Oil-Free Italian Dressing* pg. 98, using cider, rice, or white wine vinegar (to avoid discoloration.)

Cover the container and refrigerate for up to three weeks, shaking the mixture gently from time to time.

You can give jars of marinated tofu as gifts by packing the tofu into pint canning jars with springs of fresh herbs, whole dried chilies, and whole cloves of peeled garlic for decoration and flavoring. A jar of these makes a nice addition to a low-fat, vegan antipasto tray.

About Textured Vegetable Protein

Textured vegetable protein is a low-fat, dry product, used as a meat substitute. It is made from soy flour, cooked under pressure, then extruded to make different sizes and shapes. It has the advantage of being lower in fat than tofu and can take the place of frozen tofu in many recipes. Even if you object to the use of "meat substitutes" on a regular basis, textured vegetable protein can be a great transition food for people who were raised on meat and, despite the best of motives and intentions, miss their familiar foods and textures. I have had great success using textured vegetable protein in vegetarian foods for meat-loving teenagers.

Textured vegetable protein will keep for a long time, has no cholesterol, almost *no fat* and sodium, and is an excellent source of protein and fiber. It is easily rehydrated for use in soups, stews, casseroles, and sauces. The most common form available is granules, which have a ground meat-like texture. They are excellent in chilies and spaghetti sauces and can be made into burgers and "sausage" patties, (see pg. 27). I use them in egg rolls and cabbage rolls too. Textured vegetable protein can also be found in the form of flakes and chunks. All these types can be ordered by mail (see pg. 185).

Reconstituted textured vegetable protein can be made ahead of time and refrigerated for several days, or frozen for future use. The *granules* are quickly rehydrated by mixing with almost an equal amount of boiling liquid, covering, and setting aside for 5 minutes. Boiling water is usually used for reconstituting (I usually add 1 or 2 Tbsp. of soy sauce and a sprinkling of sesame meal for flavor to each cup of textured vegetable protein), but broth or tomato juice can also be used. The rule is, for each cup of textured vegetable protein granules, use ⅞ cup liquid (yields 1⅓ cups reconstituted).

Reconstituted granules and crumbled, frozen tofu (pg. 184) can be used interchangeably in many recipes. This little chart will give you the approximate yields for dry to reconstituted textured vegetable protein and its equivalent in frozen tofu. When I'm substituting for meat in a recipe, I always figure that 1 lb. of meat is equal to about 2 cups of reconstituted granules or frozen tofu in volume.

SUBSTITUTING
TEXTURED
VEGETABLE
PROTEIN FOR
FROZEN TOFU

¾ cup dry textured vegetable protein plus ½ cup + 1 Tbsp. liquid
    = 1 cup reconstituted textured vegetable protein
    = ½ lb. frozen tofu

1½ cups dry textured vegetable protein plus 1¼ cups liquid
    = 2 cup reconstituted textured vegetable protein
    = 1 lb. frozen tofu

2¼ cups dry textured vegetable protein plus 1⅞ cups liquid
    = 3 cups reconstituted textured vegetable protein
    = 1½ lb. frozen tofu

The chunks take a little longer to reconstitute, but have an amazingly meat-like texture and a pleasant, mild taste. Different marinades can be used to vary the flavor. The chunks are excellent in stews and spicy sauces, stir-fries, and kabobs.

Reconstitute the chunks by mixing 1 cup of them with 2 cups water or broth in a saucepan, bringing them to a boil, then simmering for about 15 minutes, or until the chunks are tender but not mushy. Drain and squeeze off any excess liquid, especially if the chunks are to be marinated. For a "pork" or "veal" taste, toss the reconstituted chunks with 1 tsp. sesame meal and 1 or 2 Tbsp. soy sauce (for each 1 cup dry chunks). For Crispy Chunks, see page 30. The chunks can be marinated in the *Breast of Tofu* marinade (pg. 23) or the cooking broth from the *Beefy Seitan Roast* (pg. 31), but if they (or the granules) are to be used in a spicy sauce or stew, there's no need to add flavoring or marinade. The textured vegetable protein will pick up the strong flavors.

Fat-Free "Sausage"

Makes about 10 patties

In a bowl, soak together:

1 cup dry textured vegetable protein granules
¾ cup boiling water
2 Tbsp. soy sauce

When soft, add and mix well:

½ cup reduced-fat, firm or
     medium-firm regular tofu, mashed
2 tsp. crumbled sage leaves
1 tsp. marjoram
½ tsp. garlic granules
½ tsp. onion powder
½ tsp. thyme
½ tsp. salt
½ tsp. red pepper flakes
black pepper to taste
1 tsp. liquid smoke (opt.)

When cool add:

½ cup instant gluten flour (vital wheat gluten),
     or unbleached flour.

Mix well with hands, then shape into 10 thin patties or 20 small sausage "links." Steam fry in two batches in a lightly oiled cast iron skillet over medium heat, covered, until firm and browned (7-10 minutes per side for patties; at least 20 minutes total for links.) These can be refrigerated or frozen for later use. To reheat, place in a covered, lightly oiled skillet with a few tablespoons of water, and cook over high heat until the water has evaporated.

Per patty: Calories: 66, Protein: 11 gm., Carbohydrates: 4 gm., Fat: 0 gm.

These "sausage patties" can be refrigerated or frozen and reheated in an oven or skillet or on a grill. The cooked mixture can be crumbled into other dishes.

Spicy Herb "Sausage"

Make as for *Sausage*, omitting the garlic granules, onion powder, and dried herbs. Add **2 cloves crushed garlic, ½ cup minced onion, ¼ cup minced fresh basil, ¼ cup minced fresh parsley, 1 Tbsp. minced fresh sage,** and **1 tsp. minced fresh thyme.**

Fat-Free "Italian Sausage"

Make as for *Sausage*, increasing the onion powder to 1 tsp. Omit the sage and marjoram. Add **¾ tsp. ground fennel or anise, 2 Tbsp. balsamic or red wine vinegar (or dry red wine), 1 tsp. dried oregano (or 1 Tbsp. fresh), 1 tsp. basil (or 1 Tbsp. fresh).** Use **½-1 tsp. red pepper flakes.**

Fat-Free "Ground Pork"

Make as for *Sausage*, omitting the garlic granules, onion powder, salt, black and cayenne peppers and dried herbs. Crumble and cook over low heat to use in wontons, egg rolls, and other recipes which call for ground pork.

Fat-Free "Ground Poultry"

Make as for *Sausage*, but omit the garlic powder, black and cayenne peppers, and dried herbs. Increase the onion powder to 1 tsp. and add **1 Tbsp. nutritional yeast.** Proceed as for *Fat-free "Ground Pork."*

Gluten & Seitan

**Makes almost 4 cups of raw gluten
(about 7-8 cups cooked)**

Combine in a large bowl:

**2½ cups instant gluten powder
(vital wheat gluten), pg. 179
2 cups cold water or stock**

Herbs, spices, nutritional yeast, and other flavorings may be added to the gluten powder before the water is added; part of the water may be replaced by soy sauce, miso, or tomato juice. To make seitan that is less chewy, cover the finished gluten with warm water in a bowl, and let rest for 30 minutes before using.

One cup of instant gluten powder yields 12 oz. cooked seitan, or 3 cups ground or chopped seitan (equal to 1½ lbs. beef).

Per cup: Calories: 171, Protein: 35 gm., Carbohydrates: 6 gm., Fat: 1 gm.

Cooking Gluten to Make Seitan

Note: Be careful not to boil gluten when cooking it, or it will be spongy and soft. Keep the cooking liquid at the barest simmer.

Ground Seitan

Tear or cut the raw gluten into small pieces. Slip into barely simmering cooking liquid, and simmer for 15 minutes. Cool in the liquid, then remove and squeeze each piece to remove the excess liquid. Grind in a meat or food grinder or food processor, and use in any dish calling for ground seitan. This freezes well. To make hamburger substitute, simmer in the cooking broth from *Beefy Seitan Roast*, pg. 31.

Gluten, the protein from wheat, can be cooked to make seitan, a wonderful meat substitute used to make anything from shredded barbecue to a delicious pot roast. Instant gluten powder makes preparing this very easy. If you buy "gluten flour," be sure it's vital wheat gluten and not high-gluten wheat flour sometimes used in bread baking. High-gluten wheat flour will not instantly form gluten, but will need to have the starch rinsed away.

VARIATION

Baked Gluten Balls

Form the raw gluten into ½" balls, and lay 2½" apart on lightly oiled cookie sheets. Bake at 375°F for 15-20 minutes or until quite puffy and golden brown. This makes about 96 balls. These can be frozen also. For stir-fries, you might want to slice them. They can be baked in barbecue sauce for 15 minutes for "meatless ribs."

Simmered Cutlets or Stew Chunks

Form the raw gluten into a loaf or roll. Cut into small chunks or thin cutlets, keeping in mind that the finished seitan will be twice the size after cooking. If you want the resulting cutlets to be quite thin, pound them with a mallet before simmering.

The cooking liquid you use depends on the way you want to use the seitan. You can use the cooking broth from *Beefy Seitan Roast*, (pg. 31), or *Breast of Tofu Marinade*, (pg. 22).

Have your cooking liquid simmering as you slip the cutlets or chunks into it, then turn it down so that it barely bubbles. Cover and simmer about 1 hour (45 minutes for very thin cutlets). Stir them around every so often. Cool and store in the cooking liquid. Seitan also freezes well stored in some of its cooking liquid. Excess cooking liquid can be used in soups, stews, and gravies.

Crispy Oven-Fried Seitan Chunks

Use Seitan Stew Chunks or Cutlets cut into small pieces. Roll them in *Seasoned Flour*, pg. 49, and bake them on lightly oiled, dark cookie sheets at 400°F until golden on the bottom. Turn them over and bake until golden on the other side. You can do the same with reconstituted textured vegetable protein chunks too (see pg. 26).

Beefy Seitan Roast

Serves 6-8

In a dry bowl, mix together:

> 2 cups instant gluten powder (vital wheat gluten)
> 2 Tbsp. nutritional yeast flakes
> 1 tsp. onion powder
> ½ tsp. garlic granules
> black pepper to taste

In a smaller bowl, whisk together:

> 1½ cups cold water,
>   or broth from soaking Chinese dried mushrooms
> 2 Tbsp. soy sauce or mushroom soy sauce
> 2 Tbsp. ketchup
> 2 tsp. Marmite or other yeast extract, or dark miso
> 2 tsp. Kitchen Bouquet®

Pour the broth into the gluten mixture and mix it into a ball. Place the ball into a roasting pan with a cover large enough to allow the ball to double (press the ball down to flatten a bit).

Preheat the oven to 350°F. Prepare a cooking broth made by mixing together:

> 4 cups water or broth from soaking dried Chinese
>   mushrooms
> ¼ cup ketchup
> ¼ cup soy sauce or mushroom soy sauce
> 4 tsp. Marmite or other yeast extract, or dark miso
> 4 tsp. Kitchen Bouquet®

Pour over the gluten ball, and bake uncovered for ½ hour. Prick the roast all over with a fork, and turn it over. Lower heat to 300°F and bake covered for 1 more hour, turning once in a while.

Per serving: Calories: 181, Protein: 34 gm., Carbohydrates: 9, Fat: 1 gm.

This is excellent hot or sliced cold for sandwiches. Make the whole recipe and use the leftovers for sandwiches, or grind some in a meat grinder or food processor for "hamburger." Cut some of it into strips for stir-fries and stroganoff, and/or cut thicker slices for "steaks" or "cutlets" to pan fry, grill, or broil (with or without a breading and with or without a salt-free grilling sauce, barbecue sauce, or marinade). Use the leftover cooking broth to enhance sauces.

For pot roast, during the last hour, surround the loaf with **8 potatoes, quartered, 3 medium onions,** peeled and cut into halves or quarters, and **6 carrots,** cut in 2" chunks, (use other root vegetables, if you prefer).

Make gravy by thinning the remaining cooking broth to taste with water or dry wine, and thickening it with 2 Tbsp. *Browned Flour,* pg. 49, whisked into every 2-3 cups liquid. Whisk over high heat until it boils and thickens, then simmer on low a few minutes. Add steam-fried mushrooms, if you like.

VARIATION

French-Dip Sandwiches

Layer thinly sliced, hot seitan roast inside split, French-style hard rolls. Serve with the hot cooking liquid to dip the sandwiches in while eating. If the liquid is too strong, thin each ¾ cup with ½ water and a little granulated garlic.

Tofu Cream Cheese

Makes about 1½ cups

This recipe is not difficult to do; it only takes a few minutes to make, and it's well worth it. Serve it alone or with other toppings on toast, crackers, bagels, etc.

In a small saucepan, soak for 5 minutes:

> **2 Tbsp. agar flakes**
> **or 1 tsp. agar powder**
> **2 Tbsp. cold water**
> **1 Tbsp. lemon juice**
> **½ tsp. sugar, honey, or other sweetener**

Stir over low heat until dissolved, then simmer gently for 1 minute.

Add to the pot:

> **1 (10.5 oz.) pkg. reduced-fat, extra-firm silken tofu crumbled**

Stir constantly until the tofu is hot to the touch; this is important so that the agar doesn't start firming up *before* the mixture is blended.

Pour the hot mixture into a blender with:

> **1 Tbsp. light miso**
> **1 Tbsp. sesame meal (opt.)**

You can also add any one of the following flavor variations, if you like:

- **1 clove garlic, crushed, and 1 Tbsp. fresh herbs of your choice, minced**
- **2 Tbsp. pesto**
- **2 Tbsp. fresh chives, chopped**
- **1 Tbsp. nutritional yeast, ½ tsp. onion powder, ½ tsp. garlic granules, and a pinch each of turmeric and paprika**

Blend until *very smooth*. Pour immediately into a rectangular, small, oiled or non-stick loaf pan (a 3" x 6" x 2" pan or other 2-cup container will give you a bar like 8 oz. of commercial cream cheese). Cover tightly and refrigerate until firm (about an hour).

When the loaf is firm, loosen the edges with a table knife, and invert on a plate covered with an 8" double square of cheese-cloth or clean towelling. (This will soak up any liquid that might "weep" out, which often happens to agar mixtures.) Wrap the loaf in the cheesecloth, place the whole thing in a plastic bag, and refrigerate. After a day, you can remove the cheesecloth, and store what's left in plastic wrap or a tightly sealed plastic container.

Per 2 Tbsp.: Calories: 15, Protein: 2 gm., Carbohydrates: 1 gm., Fat: 0 gm.

Tofu "Feta"

Makes 2 cups

Cut into small cubes:

> **1 lb. reduced-fat, extra-firm regular tofu,**
> **or 1½ (10.5 oz.) pkgs. extra-firm silken tofu**

Marinate in a brine of:

> **1 cup water**
> **½ cup light miso**
> **2 Tbsp. lemon juice or white wine vinegar**
> **1 tsp. salt**

Keep this refrigerated in a covered jar for up to three weeks, shaking the jar every day. Use in salads.

Per ½ cup serving: Calories: 120, Protein: 6 gm., Carbohydrates: 11 gm., Fat: 0 gm.

Bright Ideas . . .

Tofu "Cottage Cheese"

Drain some very fresh, reduced-fat, firm regular tofu; crumble and mix with *Tofu Sour Cream*, pg. 37, until it is the consistency you prefer. Add salt or light miso to taste. Mix in some chives or pineapple tidbits, if you like. Use in recipes calling for dairy cottage cheese.

Tofu "Ricotta Cheese"

This works very well in lasagne and other Italian dishes calling for ricotta cheese. Drain well some very fresh, reduced-fat firm regular tofu, and mash with a fork until it is of a fine consistency. Moisten it with a little plain, reduced-fat soymilk. Salt to taste or use a little light miso.

Tofu "Yogurt"

This is a yogurt substitute to be used in sauces, dips, dressings, etc., not necessarily to eat plain with fruit. Make *Tofu Sour Cream*, pg. 37, reducing the salt to a small pinch and using 2-4 Tbsp. lemon juice. Add as much plain, reduced-fat soymilk or water as needed to make it the consistency you prefer. This can also be used as a buttermilk substitute.

Tofu Mayonnaise

Makes 1⅓ cups

Silken tofu makes a smooth, thick, rich-tasting mayonnaise that doesn't separate easily and needs no oil.

Blend in a blender until very smooth:

1 (10.5 oz.) pkg. reduced-fat, extra-firm or firm silken tofu
1½ Tbsp. cider vinegar or lemon juice
1 tsp. sweetener of your choice (opt.)
1 tsp. salt
½ tsp. dry mustard
⅛ tsp. white pepper

This will keep about 2 weeks in the refrigerator.

Per 2 Tbsp: Calories: 13, Protein: 2 gm., Carbohydrates: 1 gm., Fat: 0 gm.

VARIATIONS

Aioli

To make a garlic dip for cold, steamed vegetables, omit the mustard and add **4 peeled garlic cloves** while blending.

Tofu "Hollandaise"

Use lemon juice instead of vinegar, and omit the mustard. Use **soft silken tofu** and heat gently just before serving. Add herbs such as dill, tarragon, or basil to taste. For a tangier sauce, add **½ tsp. cumin** and **a pinch of cayenne.**

Tartar Sauce

Add **½ cup chopped onion** and **½ cup chopped dill pickle,** with some of the pickle brine to taste. If you have no pickles, use chopped cucumber with dillweed and white wine vinegar to taste.

Tofu Sour Cream

Makes 1½ cups

Place in a blender or food processor, and process until *very smooth*:

> 1 (10.5 oz.) pkg. reduced-fat, firm or extra-firm silken tofu
> 1 Tbsp. lemon juice (you may need a bit more if using extra-firm silken tofu)
> ½ tsp. granulated sweetener or honey
> ¼ tsp. salt
> 1,000 mg. crushed vitamin C

Keep in a covered jar in the refrigerator for up to a week. Use just as you would ordinary dairy sour cream.

Per 2 Tbsp: Calories: 11, Protein: 2 gm., Carbohydrates: 0 gm., Fat: 0 gm.

Silken tofu makes any blended tofu recipe smoother and creamier than regular tofu. It blends well without the addition of liquid or oil, has a cleaner, richer taste, and contains less fat. Crushed vitamin C adds a nice tang without having to add additional lemon juice.

Soy Cheesey Gomasio

Makes 3 cups

Place in a blender and grind to a fine meal:

> 2 cups Dry-Roasted Soybeans, pg. 47
> 2 cups nutritional yeast flakes
> 2 tsp. salt
> 1 tsp. onion powder
> ½ tsp. garlic granules

Per Tbsp: Calories: 38, Protein: 4 gm., Carbohydrates: 4 gm., Fat: 1 gm.

This is a Parmesan cheese substitute that takes very little time to make and will keep for months in a covered jar in the refrigerator. The taste is not as strong as plain nutritional yeast.

Whipped Soy Cream

Makes 1¾ cups

The best-tasting replacements for whipped cream were always the ones highest in fat— until I devised this one. You can use other extracts, but I think coconut gives the mixture a rich, familiar taste.

In a small saucepan, soak for 5 minutes;

½ cup cold water
½ Tbsp. agar flakes,
   or ¼ tsp. agar powder

Bring the above mixture to a boil, and simmer for 2 minutes.

Add:

2 Tbsp. honey or other liquid sweetener
2 tsp. lemon juice

Stir this well, then add:

1 (10.5 oz.) pkg. reduced-fat, firm silken tofu, crumbled

Stir the mixture over high heat until the tofu is heated through. It should heat quickly or the agar will start to jell before the mixture is blended.

Pour the hot mixture into a blender or food processor with:

¼ tsp. coconut extract
a pinch of salt

Blend or process until the mixture is smooth and frothy (a blender works best.) Pour it into a bowl, cover, and refrigerate until it is almost cold. Whip it with a wire whisk until smooth and fluffy again. Chill until cold and softly firm like whipped cream; it will keep for several days. If any liquid separates, beat it in with a wire whisk.

Per ¼ cup: Calories: 37, Protein: 3 gm., Carbohydrates: 6 gm., Fat: 1 gm.

Tofu Milk

Makes 2 quarts

In a blender, combine until very smooth:

1 (10.5) oz. pkg. reduced-fat, firm or extra-firm silken tofu, crumbled
3 cups cold water

Add and blend again:

1 cup cold water
3 Tbsp. sweetener of your choice
1½ tsp. vanilla extract,
    or ½ tsp. almond or coconut extract (opt.)
¾ tsp. salt

Pour this into a 2-quart container, and add:

enough cold water to make 2 quarts

Stir well, pour into sterilized quart bottles, cap tightly, and refrigerate. Shake before pouring, as it tends to separate. This will keep about a week in the refrigerator.

Per cup: Calories: 40, Protein: 3 gm., Carbohydrates: 6 gm., Fat: 0 gm.

Since making your own soymilk can be time-consuming, I've devised an easy and delicious alternative which is still much cheaper than commercial, non-dairy beverages (and usually less expensive than dairy milk too, depending upon where you live). It takes only minutes to make in your blender and can be used in cooking and baking.

Plain Rice Milk

Makes about 1 quart

If you cannot use soymilk, there are commercial rice beverages for drinking and cold cereal. However, you may find them too expensive to use in cooking. This easy-to-make rice milk is excellent for use in gravies, sauces, and creamed soups, adding body and richness without fat.

Bring to a boil in a medium saucepan:

2 cups water

Add, return to a boil, reduce heat, and simmer for 45 minutes:

1 cup uncooked short grain brown rice

Combine in a blender until very smooth:

the well-cooked rice
2 cups hot water

The mixture will be thicker than dairy milk or soymilk, but may be thinned a bit with more water, if desired. It will thicken further when chilled. Store in a tightly covered, sterilized jar in the refrigerator, and shake well before using. This only keeps for 2 or 3 days.

Per cup: Calories: 108, Protein: 2 gm., Carbohydrates: 23 gm., Fat: 0 gm.

Golden Sauce

Makes 2½ cups

Cook in a small saucepan, covered:

1 cup water
1 medium potato, peeled and chunked
½ medium carrot, peeled and chunked
½ medium onion, peeled and chunked

When the carrot is tender, add the cooked vegetables to a blender along with:

½ cup reduced-fat, firm or medium-firm regular tofu, crumbled
1-4 Tbsp. nutritional yeast (½ cup if using as melted "cheese")
1 Tbsp. lemon juice
1 tsp. salt,
    or 1 Tbsp. light miso + ½ tsp. salt
¼ tsp. garlic granules

Blend until very smooth. Serve immediately or refrigerate (it will keep for a week and can be gently reheated).

Per ¼ cup: Calories: 36, Protein: 2 gm., Carbohydrates: 6 gm., Fat: 0 gm.

Tangy Cream Sauce

Makes 2 cups

Make the *Golden Sauce*, omitting the carrot and blending with the tofu:

2 Tbsp. sesame meal

Per ¼ cup: Calories: 48, Protein: 3 gm., Carbohydrates: 6 gm., Fat: 1 gm.

Use like a cheddar cheese sauce. It's great on steamed vegetables and macaroni. You can also spread it on toast and broil it for a "grilled cheese" sandwich, or spread it on top of casseroles and broil.

VARIATION

Using the smaller amount of yeast this can be used as a rich béchamel (cream) sauce; with more yeast, it's like a white cheese sauce. It's delicious on steamed vegetables, broiled on toast or broiled on top of lasagne, canneloni, or moussaka.

Yeast Gravy

Makes about 2½ cups

There are many variations of this recipe, but this is my standard, fat-free take on it, and very popular it is! It's excellent on potatoes, rice, tofu, seitan, biscuits, and much, much more.

Whisk in a heavy saucepan over high heat:

⅓ cup unbleached all-purpose or whole wheat pastry flour

When the flour smells toasty, remove from the heat and whisk in:

2½ cups water
⅓ cup nutritional yeast flakes
2 Tbsp. soy sauce
½ tsp. salt

Place over high heat again, and stir until it thickens and comes to a boil. Reduce the heat and cook for 2-5 minutes.

This keeps well in the refrigerator for a week. It will thicken up when chilled, so you'll probably have to add a bit of water when reheating. For variety, try making this with *Browned Flour*, pg. 49, substitute dry white or red wine or mushroom cooking or soaking liquid for half the water, or add fresh or dried chopped herbs, steam-fried mushrooms, steam-fried onions, crumbled *Fat-Free "Sausage,"* ground seitan, crushed fresh garlic, or ¼ tsp. garlic granules. For a giblet-style gravy, add 1 cup chopped seitan or prepared textured vegetable protein chunks.

Per ¼ cup: Calories: 27, Protein: 2 gm., Carbohydrates: 4 gm., Fat: 0 gm.

Brown Gravy

Makes about 2½ cups

If you don't have any nutritional yeast, try this good gravy.

In a small saucepan or skillet, steam-fry:

¼ cup regular or non-alcoholic dry white wine
1 small onion, minced
2 cloves garlic, minced
1 cup fresh mushrooms, sliced (opt.)

When all the liquid has evaporated and the onion is soft, remove from the heat and whisk in:

½ cup Browned Flour, pg. 49
2 cups vegetarian broth
¼ cup regular or non-alcoholic dry white wine

Stir constantly over high heat until bubbly and thickened. Lower the heat and cook for 2-5 minutes. Add a little water if it's too thick and salt and pepper to taste.

For variety, try any of the suggestions under the *Yeast Gravy* recipe, pg. 42.

Per ½ cup: Calories: 54, Protein: 4 gm., Carbohydrates: 9 gm., Fat: 0 gm.

Basic Barbecue Sauce

Makes about 5 cups

Feel free to experiment with this barbecue sauce recipe. Try coffee, fruit juice, wine, or beer instead of the water; use molasses or brown sugar instead of honey, use vinegar (any kind) instead of lemon juice; use red chile flakes, chopped, pickled jalapeños, or canned chile chipoltes in adobado sauce (smoked chiles in red chile sauce) instead of chile powder and Tabasco; add some liquid smoke, soy sauce, Chinese chile paste, . . . the possibilities are endless!

Mix together well in a large pot, and simmer for 15-30 minutes:

3 cups water
1 medium onion, chopped and steam-fried
1 (6 oz.) can tomato paste
¾ cup lemon juice
⅓ cup honey
¼ cup Sesame Meal, pg. 47
2 Tbsp. garlic granules
4 tsp. salt
4 tsp. paprika
4 tsp. chile powder
1 Tbsp. prepared mustard
1½ tsp. cinnamon
1½ tsp. allspice
1 tsp. Vegetarian Worcestershire Sauce, pg. 48
¼ tsp. pepper
¼ tsp. Tabasco sauce

Per ½ cup: Calories: 69, Protein: 1 gm., Carbohydrates: 14 gm., Fat: 1 gm.

Mock Hollandaise Sauce

Makes 2½ cups

In a small, heavy saucepan, mix together:

¾ cup cold water
¼ cup fine yellow cornmeal or corn flour

Stir constantly over high heat until boiling, then turn down to medium heat, and cook, stirring constantly, for 5 minutes.

Place the cooked mixture in a blender with:

1¼ cups hot water
½ cup reduced-fat, firm or medium-firm regular tofu, crumbled
1 Tbsp. lemon juice
1½ tsp. salt
1 tsp. onion powder
¼ tsp. garlic granules
pinch paprika
pinch turmeric

Blend this until very smooth. Heat gently before serving. This can be refrigerated for up to a week. If desired, you can add chopped fresh chives, dill, or other fresh herbs, 1 Tbsp. *Sesame Meal*, pg. 47, or 1 tsp. ground cumin (dry-roasted first, if possible) and 1 tsp. chile paste.

Per ½ cup: Calories: 46, Protein: 3 gm., Carbohydrates: 7 gm., Fat: 0 gm.

Yellow cornmeal can be used in many instances to provide a "buttery" flavor —here's one excellent example. Pulverize the cornmeal in a dry blender if you can only get a coarse variety.

Corn Butter

Makes about 1½ cups

If you miss a melty spread to put on your toast, vegetables, or potatoes, look no further. This even works well for cinnamon toast, one of my favorite comfort foods. Pulverize the cornmeal in a dry blender if you can only get a coarse variety.

Mix together in a small, heavy saucepan:

¾ cup cold water

4 Tbsp. fine yellow cornmeal or corn flour

Cook over medium-high heat, stirring constantly until the mixture is quite thick. Cover and cook over low heat for 5 minutes more.

Scrape into a blender with a spatula, and add to the blender:

¾ cup reduced-fat, extra-firm silken or medium-firm regular tofu, well drained

¼ cup water

¾ tsp. salt

Blend until very smooth. Pour into a tightly covered, wide mouth container, and refrigerate. This firms up nicely when chilled and melts well on hot food.

Corn butter lasts for about 5 days, so I only make this small amount. You can double the recipe, if you like.

Per Tbsp.: Calories: 8, Protein: 1 gm., Carbohydrates: 1 gm., Fat: 0 gm.

VARIATION

Garlic Butter

This can be broiled on toast, spread on crispy, baked potato skins, steamed greens, or tossed with pasta. To the basic *Corn Butter* mixture, blend in **½ Tbsp. nutritional yeast flakes, 2 cloves garlic, peeled, or 1 tsp. garlic granules, ½ tsp. onion powder, ½ tsp. dry herbs, or 1 Tbsp. fresh herbs, and ¼ tsp. salt**

Sesame Meal

Makes a generous 2 cups

Place in a heavy, dry skillet over high heat:

2 cups hulled, raw sesame seeds

Stir constantly until the seeds turn golden-beige and start to pop. Remove from the heat, and cool slightly. Pour the seeds into a blender, and blend at high speed, stopping and stirring from the bottom a few times, until the consistency of fine meal (but not a paste). Keep in a covered container in the freezer.

Per tsp.: Calories: 16, Protein: 1 gm., Carbohydrates: 0 gm., Fat: 2 gm.

Sesame seeds may be high in fat, but when roasted and ground into meal, a little goes a long way. Sprinkle lightly on top of pasta, casseroles, and vegetables. I make up this amount every so often and keep it in the freezer so that I always have it on hand.

Bright Idea . . .

Dry-Roasted Soybeans ("Soynuts") and Chick-peas

Keep a supply of both of these on hand in the freezer to use for snacks or in recipes in place of nuts and seeds.

Soak dry soybeans or chick-peas in enough water to cover overnight. Drain, rinse, and place in a pot with enough fresh water to cover. Bring to a boil, turn down, and simmer for 10 minutes. Drain.

Spread the beans in a single layer on lightly oiled cookie sheets. Roast at 350°F for about 45 minutes or until golden and crispy all over, stirring several times while roasting. Cool thoroughly, then store in plastic bags or containers in the freezer.

Vegetarian Worcestershire Sauce

Makes about 2 cups

This is good!

Combine in a blender:

1 cup cider vinegar
⅓ cup dark molasses
¼ cup soy sauce or mushroom soy sauce
¼ cup water
3 Tbsp. lemon juice
1½ Tbsp. salt
1½ tsp. powdered mustard
1 tsp. onion powder
¾ tsp. powdered ginger
½ tsp. black pepper
¼ tsp. garlic granules,
¼ tsp. cayenne
¼ tsp. cinnamon
⅛ tsp. ground cloves or allspice
⅛ tsp. ground cardamom

Pour into a saucepan and bring to a boil. Store in a jar in the refrigerator.

Per Tbsp.: Calories: 10, Protein: 0 gm., Carbohydrates: 3 gm., Fat: 0 gm.

Bright Idea . . .

Non-stick Cooking Blend

Use this for greasing baking pans instead of using vegetable shortening or non-stick spray. Blend together ½ cup soy lecithin (liquid) and 1 cup canola oil. Keep in a covered container in the refrigerator. Apply a thin coat when needed. If you don't have non-stick skillets or pots, use a little of this on the bottom of the pan before cooking.

Seasoned Flour

Makes a scant 2½ cups

Mix together:

2 cups whole wheat flour or other grain flour
¼ cup nutritional yeast flakes
1 tsp. salt
1 tsp. onion powder (opt.)
pepper to taste

Store in a tightly covered container in the refrigerator.

Per Tbsp.: Calories: 23, Protein: 1 gm., Carbohydrates: 4 gm., Fat: 0 gm.

I use whole wheat flour here not only for its nutritional value, but its taste—white flour just doesn't produce the same results. If you are allergic to wheat, substitute brown rice, spelt, teff, or kamut flours, or use crumbs made from a natural, crispy, brown rice cereal or fine cornmeal.

Bright Idea . . .

Browned Flour

I keep Browned Flour in a plastic container in my freezer at all times. Use it for thickening gravies and stews—wherever you would have used a brown roux (made from flour and fat) before.

Place unbleached flour in a dry, heavy skillet (cast iron is the best). Stir constantly with a wooden spoon over high heat until the flour starts to turn color. If it's browning too fast, turn the heat down. Pay extra attention to the edges of the pan, scraping this part often. You can brown your flour to a golden beige or light brown—just be careful not to burn it.

Cool the flour before storing. You can use it directly from the freezer.

Seasoned Coating Mix

Makes 1⅓ cups

This coating mixture is useful for tofu slices, sliced, oven-baked vegetables, such as zucchini or eggplant, and seitan cutlets (see pg. 30). Keep some ready for use in your refrigerator.

Mix together:

> **1 cup soft whole wheat bread crumbs**
> **   or finely crumbled, whole grain cold cereal**
> **¼ cup cornmeal**
> **2 tsp. paprika**
> **1 tsp. salt (herbal or seasoned, if desired)**
> **½ tsp. black pepper**
> **½ tsp. ground sage**
> **½ tsp. dried thyme**
> **½ tsp. dried basil**

Store in a tightly covered container in the refrigerator.

Per Tbsp.: Calories: 20, Protein: 1 gm., Carbohydrates: 4 gm., Fat: 0 gm.

VARIATION

Breaded Slices

Dip tofu, vegetable, or seitan slices in **1 cup reduced-fat soy-milk** mixed with **1 Tbsp. lemon juice**. Dredge in *Seasoned Coating Mix*. Place on greased, dark cookie sheets, and bake at 400°F until golden on the bottom. Turn the slices over and bake until golden on the other side.

Chapter 2

Appetizers, Snacks & Sandwiches

You can give skeptical friends their first taste of flavorful, almost fat-free, vegetarian foods when you serve "fun foods" such as *Layered "Texas" Bean Dip*, *Quesadillas*, or *Tofu Onion Dip*.

If lunches are a problem (aren't they always—no matter what your diet?), you'll find dozens of ideas for making bag lunches appealing and nourishing, and hot, at-home lunches anything but boring (don't forget to check out the soups in Chapter 4 too!).

Pita Crisps

Makes 6 to 8 dozen crisps

These crispy tri-angles are perfect for dips that are too thick for tortilla chips.

Split in half to make 12 rounds:

6 whole wheat pita breads

Mist with water and sprinkle with salt (you can also sprinkle them with garlic salt or seasoned salts). Stack the rounds and cut them into 6 or 8 wedges. Places the wedges in single layers on cookie sheets. Bake at 400°F until crisp and golden, about 5 minutes. Cool on racks.

Per pita: Calories: 150, Protein: 6 gm., Carbohydrates: 28 gm., Fat: 0 gm.

Water-Crisped Tortilla Chips

Makes about 8 cups

There are some baked tortilla chips on the market now, but if you can't find them in your area, try making your own. They're great with salsa, bean dip, and guacamole, and almost any other dip as well.

Dip in water one at a time:

12 corn tortillas

Let them drain briefly on a rack, and sprinkle the tops lightly with salt. Cut each tortilla into 6 or 8 wedges. Fill up ungreased cookie sheets with single layers of the wedges, close together but not over-lapping. Bake at 400°F for about 7 or 8 minutes. The chips should be crispy when cooled. Cool them completely before storing in an airtight container.

Per ¾ cup serving: Calories: 65, Protein: 2 gm., Carbohydrates: 12 gm., Fat: 1 gm.

Tofu Onion Dip

Makes about 1½ cups

Combine in a blender until very smooth:

> **1 (10.5 oz.) pkg. reduced-fat, extra-firm silken tofu,
> or 8 oz. reduced-fat, firm regular tofu**
> **2 Tbsp. lemon juice**
> **¼ tsp. salt**

If the mixture seems difficult to blend, add a few tablespoons of water.

Add and blend again

> **½ (1 oz.) packet vegetarian onion soup mix**

If you don't want to use soup mix, add in:

> **2 tsp. yeast extract**
> **1¼ tsp. brown sugar,
> or 2 tsp. maple syrup**
> **1 tsp. soy sauce**
> **2 Tbsp. dried onion flakes**
> **¼ tsp. garlic granules**
> **½ tsp. Vegetarian Worcestershire Sauce, pg. 48
> (opt.)**

Place the mixture in a serving bowl or covered container, and refrigerate for several hours to blend the flavors.

Per 2 Tbsp.: Calories: 12, Protein: 1 gm., Carbohydrates: 1 gm., Fat: 0 gm.

If you use a commercial onion soup mix, be sure it contains no animal products.

Bean Dip

Makes 3½-4 cups

This is delicious either hot or room temperature with baked tortilla chips, and also makes a great stand-in for fatty refried beans in recipes for tacos, enchiladas, etc. Try this on baked potatoes too.

Puree in a food processor:

4 cups well-cooked beans (pintos, black beans, or red beans), drained (2-16 oz. cans)
½ cup onion, minced
1-2 Tbsp. cider or wine vinegar
1 tsp. salt
1 tsp. ground cumin
1 tsp. dry oregano
3 cloves garlic, crushed,
   or 1 tsp. garlic granules
1 tsp. chile powder
dash pepper
a few sprinkles of Louisiana hot sauce
a few shakes of liquid smoke (opt.)

Place in a covered container, and refrigerate. Bring to room temperature or heat gently before serving. If you prefer a milder onion and garlic flavor, first steam-fry the onion and garlic in a bit of water until softened. For a more intense flavor, first dry-roast the cumin, oregano, and chile powder in a heavy, dry skillet for a few seconds—do not scorch.

Per 2 Tbsp.: Calories: 35, Protein: 2 gm., Carbohydrates: 7 gm., Fat: 0 gm.

VARIATION

For a delicious change, omit the chile powder, pepper and hot sauce. Instead, add 2 tsp. canned chile chipotle (smoked jalapeño chile in tomato sauce).

Layered "Texas" Bean Dip

You've probably had a version of this at a party or two, a fat-laden but delicious concoction (sometimes called "Texas Dip") consisting of layers of canned, refried beans (with lard), avocados or guacamole, sour cream (sometimes mixed with mayonnaise), chili sauce, olives, and grated cheese. Your guests will love our fat-free version.

Spread ½ recipe **Bean Dip** (made with pinto or black beans) in an 8" round on a large platter. Leaving about ½" of beans showing at the edge, top with a circle made of ⅓ recipe **Low-Fat Guacamole**, pg. 60, and **1 cup tomato salsa (opt.)**. Top this with 1 recipe **Tofu Sour Cream**, pg. 37. Sprinkle the top with **1 cup red or yellow bell pepper, chopped, ¼ cup green onion, chopped**, and **2 Tbsp. vegetarian bacon bits (opt.)**. Decorate with **fresh cilantro** and surround with **Water-Crisped Tortilla Chips**, pg. 52, or commercial, baked tortilla chips for scooping up the dip. This makes 6-8 servings.

Bright Idea . . .

Nachos

Spread *Water-Crisped Tortilla Chips*, pg. 52, or commercial, baked tortilla chips in a single layer on a cookie sheet. Dot with *Bean Dip*, pg. 54, chopped onion, and slices of pickled jalapeño peppers, if desired. Heat in a 350°F oven until hot and crispy. Dribble with hot *Golden Sauce* or *Tangy Cream Sauce*, pg. 41, and serve with tomato salsa, *Tofu Sour Cream*, pg. 37, *Low-Fat Guacamole*, pg. 60, or chopped fresh cilantro, if desired.

Dill Dip

Makes about 1¼ cups

This is perfect for dipping raw vegetables.

Combine in a blender until very smooth:

> 1 (10.5 oz.) pkg. reduced-fat, firm silken tofu
> 3 Tbsp. lemon juice
> 1 tsp. dry dillweed,
>   or 1-2 Tbsp. fresh dillweed, chopped
> 1 tsp. dry basil,
>   or 1 Tbsp. fresh basil, chopped
> ½ tsp. salt
> ½ tsp. sugar or sweetener of your choice
> ¼ tsp. onion powder
> ¼ tsp. garlic granules
> pinch cayenne pepper (opt.)

Per 2 Tbsp. serving: Calories: 15, Protein: 2 gm., Carbohydrates: 1 gm., Fat: 1 gm.

Bright Idea . . .

Dips

You can convert any dip recipe that calls for mayonnaise, sour cream, cream cheese, etc., by substituting *Tofu Sour Cream*, pg. 37, or *Tofu Mayonnaise*, pg. 36, for the dairy ingredients. These two versatile tofu mixtures can also be flavored for dipping by adding any of the following to taste: herbal salt, pureed, roasted red peppers, soaked, dried tomatoes with fresh herbs, onion flakes, etc.

Devilled Tofu (Eggless Salad)

Makes 3 cups

Use this as you would egg salad in sandwiches, on crackers, or celery sticks.

Drain and pat dry:

2 (10.5 oz.) pkgs. reduced-fat, extra-firm silken tofu, or 1 lb. reduced-fat, firm regular tofu

Cut it into small cubes, and steam in a colander or collapsible steamer over hot water for 5 minutes. Drain well and mix with:

½ cup Tofu Mayonnaise, pg. 36
2 green onions, chopped,
   or ¼ cup white or red onion, chopped
1 stalk celery, minced
½ small green or red bell pepper, chopped (opt.)
2 Tbsp. nutritional yeast flakes
1 Tbsp. Sesame Meal, pg. 47
2 Tbsp. dill pickle, chopped (opt.)
½ Tbsp. prepared mustard
2 tsp. dry dillweed,
   or a heaping Tbsp. fresh dillweed, chopped
2 tsp. turmeric
1 clove garlic, pressed,
   or ¼ tsp. garlic granules
paprika, salt, and pepper to taste

Mash the tofu coarsely with a fork as you mix with the other ingredients. Refrigerate in a covered bowl.

Per ½ cup: Calories: 60, Protein: 8 gm., Carbohydrates: 3 gm., Fat: 1 gm.

Baked Pâté

Makes two 3" x 6" x 2" loaves (16 servings)

The original version of this pâté, made with oil and sunflower seeds, is all the rage in my area. I love it, so I made a low-fat version, using tofu and roasted soybeans or garbanzos. You can make it less spicy, if you wish, and it freezes well. Best of all, it's a cinch to make.

Combine in a blender until smooth:

½ cup warm water or vegetarian broth
1 medium onion, peeled and chunked
1 large russet potato, peeled and chunked
½ cup Dry-Roasted Soybeans or Garbanzos, pg. 47
4 oz. reduced-fat, firm regular tofu, drained and
    crumbled
½ cup whole wheat flour
½ cup nutritional yeast flakes
¼ cup soy sauce
2 cloves garlic, peeled,
    or ¼ tsp. garlic granules
½ tsp. dried thyme
½ tsp. savory or marjoram
½ tsp. oregano
½ tsp. basil
½ tsp. rosemary
½ tsp. tarragon
½ tsp. nutmeg
½ tsp. allspice
pepper to taste

Fresh herbs can be used instead of the dried herbs; just increase the quantity to 1 tsp. of each. Pour the mixture into two non-stick 3" x 6" x 2" loaf pans (fruitcake pans), and bake at 350°F for 1 hour.

Cool the pans on a rack, then carefully remove the pâté from the pans by loosening the edges with a knife, then inverting on a plate. Wrap and refrigerate for up to a week (or cut into whatever size is useful for you, wrap well with foil or plastic, and freeze for up to 3 months). This is good spread on rye crisp, melba toast, wheat toast, or pita crisps, or in celery sticks. Or you can slice it to use in sandwiches (with gourmet mustard), or serve on a bed of lettuce.

Per serving: Calories: 65, Protein: 5 gm., Carbohydrates: 9 gm., Fat: 1 gm.

Pâté Variations

VARIATIONS

—Omit the pepper from the recipe. Sprinkle **coarse black pepper** on the bottoms of the loaf pans before adding the batter.

—Add some **chopped, roasted bell pepper** or **well-drained pimiento** to the batter.

—Use **dry white wine** instead of broth or water.

—Omit ¼ cup of water or broth, and use **¼ cup brandy** instead.

—Add some **chopped fresh parsley**.

Low-Fat Guacamole

Makes 2 cups

I have to admit that I absolutely love avocados (I grew up in California, where we often had lunches of ripe avocados with sourdough bread), so doing without guacamole is somewhat of a trial for me. I tried a lot of low-fat guacamoles ("mole" means a sort of mashed-up mixture, so I think it's fair to call this mixture guacamole). Then I came up with this tasty version.

Cook in a little water until tender:

1 (10 oz.) pkg. whole small green beans, frozen

Drain well. Place in a food processor and process until smooth.

Add:

½ (10.5 oz.) pkg. reduced-fat, extra-firm silken tofu, or ½ cup reduced-fat, firm or medium-firm regular tofu

Process again. When smooth, add and pulse:

¼ cup tomato salsa
2 Tbsp. lemon juice
1 tsp. soy sauce
½ tsp salt
½ tsp. ground cumin
½ tsp. garlic granules

Cool and refrigerate. Serve with oven-crisped tortilla.

Per ¼ cup serving: Calories: 21, Protein: 2 gm., Carbohydrates: 3 gm., Fat: 0 gm.

Tofu Shakes

Serves 2

This is delicious and thick—great for breakfast, snacks, or dessert.

Combine in a blender until smooth:

1 frozen banana (peeled before freezing), cut in chunks
1 cup orange juice or other fruit juice
⅓ (10.5 oz.) pkg. soft silken tofu,
**   or 4 oz. reduced-fat, medium-firm regular tofu**
a handful of berries or other fresh or frozen fruit (opt.)

Per serving: Calories: 129, Protein: 5 gm., Carbohydrates: 26 gm., Fat: 1 gm.

Blender Fruit Shake

Serves 1

You can have a thick, creamy shake without dairy or even soy.

Combine in a blender until smooth:

¾ cup fruit juice of your choice
half a frozen banana (peeled before freezing), cut in chunks
a few berries or a chunk of any other fresh or frozen fruit

Per serving: Calories: 168, Protein: 2 gm., Carbohydrates: 38 gm., Fat: 0 gm.

Bright Idea . . .

Quesadillas

"Quesadillas" (pronounced kay-sah-*dee*-yahs) were originally little cheese and corn dough turnovers from Mexico. Now they refer to almost any filling inside a folded corn or wheat tortilla, baked, grilled, or fried. Whichever way they are cooked, they make a delicious snack or light meal.

For each quesadilla, spread one half of a tortilla with some *Bean Dip*, pg. 54. Fold the other half over, and either bake on a cookie sheet at 500°F for about 5-7 minutes, (until crispy), pan-fry them in a hot, dry, heavy skillet until crispy on both sides, or grill over hot coals until crispy on both sides. Serve with tomato salsa, and *Tofu Sour Cream*, pg. 37.

Other additions to the quesadilla filling might be *Golden* or *Tangy Cream Sauce*, pg. 41, chopped tomato, onion, bell pepper, or hot peppers, fresh cilantro (chopped), or canned beans (mashed or cooked) with some hot sauce, or any favorite taco, enchilada, or burrito filling, such as on pg. 126. Other toppings for quesadillas might be *Golden Sauce, Tangy Cream Sauce*, pg. 41, or *Low-Fat Guacamole*, pg. 60.

Chick-pea Sandwich Filling

Yield: 3 cups

This simple mixture will become a sandwich staple.

Mix in a bowl:

**2 cups cooked chick-peas (1-16 oz. can), well-
drained and coarsely mashed with a fork
½ cup celery, chopped
3 green onions, chopped
¾ cup Tofu Mayonnaise, pg. 36
salt and pepper to taste**

You can add chopped green or red bell pepper, chopped dill pickle, hot chutney, sunflower sprouts, and/or a bit of curry powder if you like.

Per ½ cup: Calories: 111, Protein: 6 gm., Carbohydrates: 17 gm., Fat: 2 gm.

Bright Idea . . .

Vegetarian Hero or Gyro

Use a loaf of French or sourdough bread, cut in half length-wise and hollowed out, filled with sliced Roma tomatoes, red onion, romaine lettuce, roasted or grilled eggplant, and peppers. Optional items: *Tofu Mayonnaise*, pg. 36, *Smoky Baked Tofu*, pg. 24, fresh parsley and/or basil, gourmet mustard, grilled mushrooms, *Seitan Roast*, pg. 31, or commercial vegetarian "deli slices."

Sandwich Ideas

Cold Sandwiches

Breast of Tofu, pg. 23, (in slices or chopped up) with *Tofu Mayonnaise*, pg. 36,—add pickles, celery, peppers, whatever you like

Savory Tofu Dinner Loaf pg. 105, use leftover slices

Beefy Seitan Roast, pg. 31, thin, cold slices with *Tofu Mayonnaise*, pg.36, and Dijon mustard

Best-Ever Tofu Burgers, pg. 124

Chick-pea Sandwich Filling, pg. 63

Devilled Tofu, pg. 57

Baked Pâté, pg. 58, sliced

commercial vegetarian "deli slices"

Smoky Baked Tofu slices, pg. 24

Tofu Cream Cheese, pg. 33, with jam, jelly, marmalade, dried fruit, etc.

Fat-Free "Sausage," pg. 37, cold

Tofu Mayonnaise, pg. 36, with sliced Roma tomatoes and lettuce

Bright Idea . . .

Bread options

Instead of sliced wheat bread, try Armenian bread,English muffins, French or Italian bread, sliced or as hard rolls, pita bread, rye crisp, *Savory Hamburger Rolls*, pg. 82, tortillas, or water bagels.

Hot Sandwiches

steamed broccoli or asparagus with *Tangy Cream Sauce*, pg. 41, in pita bread

roasted or grilled eggplant, peppers and/or mushrooms on toast, in a tortilla or in French bread with *Tangy Cream Sauce*, pg. 41

Beefy Seitan Roast, pg. 31, thin slices, hot on French bread with the juices to dip in, or hot on soft bread with *Yeast Gravy*, pg. 42

hot *Breaded Breast of Tofu*, pg. 23, on toast with *Yeast Gravy*, pg. 42

Savory Tofu Dinner Loaf, pg. 105, reheated slices on toast or a toasted bun, bagel, or English muffin with ketchup, onions, etc.

Fat-Free "Sausage," pg. 27, or *Best-Ever Tofu Burgers*, pg. 124,

Golden or *Tangy Cream Sauce*, pg. 41, grilled, open-faced with tomato on toast

Quesadillas, pg. 62

pita or English muffin pizzas

Steam-fried mushrooms on toast (can add a sauce, such as gravy, *Tangy Cream Sauce*, pg. 41)

Bright Idea . . .

Other Bag Lunch Ideas

Instead of sandwiches for lunch, try *Southern "Fried" Tofu*, pg.110, cold pizza, hearty grain, potato, or pasta salads, chef's salad with vegetables, fruits, cold *Baked Breast of Tofu* or *Smoky Baked Tofu*, pg. 24, marinated artichokes, etc., leftover soups, stews, bean mixtures, chili on pasta in a wide-mouth thermos, carrot and celery sticks marinated in leftover dill pickle brine, tofu or bean dip with raw veggies, *Baked Pâté*, pg. 58, in celery sticks.

Bright Idea . . .

Filled Pitas and Tortilla Roll-ups

Pita bread pockets and rolled-up wheat tortillas make common foods into interesting picnic lunch fare. Here are some filling ideas—I'm sure you can think of lots more:

Chick-pea Sandwhich Filling, pg. 63
Breast of Tofu, pg. 22, or *Smoky Baked Tofu*, pg. 24,
       chopped up with *Tofu Mayonaise* pg. 36
steamed broccoli, cauliflower, asparagus, or other veg
       etables in hot *Golden* or *Tangy Cream Sauce*, pg.
       41
any kind of hearty salad
roasted vegetables with *Tangy Cream Sauce*, pg. 41
chiles, stews, and bean mixtures

You get the idea!

Bright Idea . . .

Toast Crust Tarts

For an easy, crispy crust for savory tarts, cut the crusts from slices of bread, roll very thinly with a rolling pin, and fit them into the bottom and sides of non-stick muffin cups. Fill with any baked fillings used in quiches, filled breads, mushrooms in a sauce, stews, chiles, or steamed vegetables in *Tangy Cream Sauce*, pg. 41, etc. Bake at 350°F for 30 minutes. Remove from the cups and serve hot or cold. You can also bake these unfilled for about 20 minutes or until golden brown, and fill after they have cooled on racks.

Chapter 3
Breakfast Dishes
And Breads

I've changed my thinking on breakfast somewhat over the years—I used to be a fan of the hearty, "nutritionally balanced" breakfast (my adult children will attest to this, probably with groans!). The years must have mellowed me, because I now believe that everyone has to follow his or her own natural pattern for breakfast. Some people just can't eat until about 10 a.m.; some people like their biggest meal in the morning; others want just fruit until lunch time—it's very individual and no one way is the right way. I do not recommend "sugar and caffeine" breakfasts of coffee and sweet rolls or doughnuts, however. This type of snack will give you a "high," closely followed by a crashing "low." If you just can't face a substantial breakfast, stick to fruit, or at least Swiss water-decaffeinated coffee with toast made from good bread.

This chapter has something for everyone—a rice and tofu "yogurt," vegan, fat-free pancakes lighter than you can imagine, eggless "scramble," muffins, and sweet breads. If you're planning a brunch, there's plenty of material here for menu-planning, but check Chapter 1 for *Fat-Free "Sausages"* and Chapter 7 for some scrumptious potato dishes.

I've included breads in this chapter, because they so often serve as the main breakfast dish. I've had a great time devising fat-free versions of old favorites, such as *Cinnamon Sticky Buns*, pg. 82. I love to bake bread, and I hope you'll give it a try. Yeasted breads can replace high-fat quick breads and pastries, offering better nutrition and the same home-baked satisfaction.

Basic Pancakes

**Makes about 24 four-inch pancakes
(or 3-4 dozen small pancakes)**

The fruit juice I use here results in a perfect pancake. You can just use apple juice, vary the flavor with orange juice (try freshly-squeezed with some grated orange rind added), or try any favorite juice of your choice. A little soymilk powder or soy flour adds protein to this breakfast dish.

In a large bowl, mix together:

2½ cups whole wheat pastry flour, unbleached white flour, or a combination

¼ cup reduced-fat soymik powder or low-fat soy flour (opt.)

4 tsp. baking powder

2 tsp. baking soda

1 tsp. salt

When the dry ingredients are well-combined, stir in:

3 cups fruit juice (apple, orange, etc.)

Mix briefly—lumps are okay.

Heat a non-stick griddle or skillet (or a heavy skillet lightly greased with an oiled cloth) over high heat until it is hot; then turn it down to medium high. Spoon the batter onto the pan, making 2"-4" (silver dollar) pancakes. When the tops are bubbly, turn them over carefully and cook until the under-side is golden and the middle is cooked (you can spread apart one pancake using a fork to test). Serve immediately with maple syrup or other toppings.

Per pancake: Calories: 57, Protein: 2 gm., Carbohydrates: 12 gm., Fat: 0 gm.

Egg-Free French Toast

Makes 6 slices of toast

You won't miss all the butter and eggs usually associated with this breakfast dish—it's delicious!

Have ready:

6 slices whole wheat bread

Blend or whisk together in a shallow bowl:

1 cup reduced-fat soymilk
2 Tbsp. flour
1 Tbsp. nutritional yeast flakes
1 tsp. sugar or sweetener of your choice
1 tsp. vanilla
½ tsp. salt
pinch of nutmeg

Dip the bread slices into this mixture, and cook either on a non-stick griddle until browned on both sides, or on a greased cookie sheet in a 400°F oven until golden on both sides, turning once. For an interesting change of pace, bake the French toast in a non-stick waffle iron until golden-brown.

Serve with maple syrup or your favorite topping.

Per slice: Calories: 80, Protein: 4 gm., Carbohydrates: 13 gm., Fat: 1 gm.

Banana French Toast

VARIATION

Omit ½ cup soymilk and the flour, and blend the remaining ingredients with **1 ripe banana**.

Rice and Tofu "Yogurt"

Makes 1¾ cups

This is good poured over fruit or muesli. Crushed vitamin C adds a nice tang without increasing the lemon juice.

Combine in a blender until very smooth:

1 cup cold cooked rice (short grain brown rice is best)
⅔ cup cold water
½ (10.5 oz.) pkg. reduced-fat, extra-firm silken tofu
¼ cup frozen apple or pineapple juice concentrate
2 Tbsp. lemon juice
1 tsp. non-dairy acidophilus powder
½ tsp. light or white miso
1000 mg. vitamin C, crushed

This will keep refrigerated in a covered jar for several days.

Per ½ cup: Calories: 120, Protein: 5 gm., Carbohydrates: 24 gm., Fat: 1 gm.

Fruit "Yogurt"

VARIATION

After blending, add **1 cup sliced, frozen berries** or other fruit, and blend briefly.

Tofu "Bacon"

Makes about 40 thin slices

Mix together in a shallow container:

½ cup soy sauce (low-salt, if available)
1 Tbsp. nutritional yeast flakes
1 Tbsp. maple syrup
½ Tbsp. liquid smoke

With a cheese slicer, shave into very thin slices:

½ lb. reduced-fat, extra-firm regular tofu

Marinate the tofu in the soy sauce mixture for 1 day or more. To cook, heat a lightly oiled, heavy skillet or non-stick griddle over medium high heat. When the pan is hot, "fry" the tofu slices until they are golden-brown and almost crispy on both sides, scraping underneath the slices as you turn them with a sturdy spatula. Turn several times during cooking, and cool in the pan (it crisps up as it cools).

This makes excellent "BLT" sandwiches and can be sliced or diced and added to other dishes for a bacon flavor.

Per slice: Calories: 9, Protein: 1 gm., Carbohydrates: 1 gm., Fat: 0 gm.

It's hard to make a product that is crispy like bacon without frying it in oil, but this comes close. If you want it to be crunchier, you can dry it in an electric home food dehydrator.

Scrambled Tofu

Serves 1

This versatile dish need not be confined to breakfast—it can be a stand-by for any meal just like scrambled eggs, but with about one-fifth of the fat!

Crumble coarsely in a small bowl:
   **½ (10.5 oz.) pkg. reduced-fat, extra-firm silken tofu,
      or 4 oz. reduced-fat, medium-firm regular tofu**

Sprinkle with:
   1 Tbsp. nutritional yeast flakes

Stir gently to coat.

In a cup, whisk together:
   **1 Tbsp. water
   1½ tsp. light miso, ¼ tsp. salt, or 1 tsp. soy sauce
   ⅛ tsp. turmeric
   ⅛ tsp. onion powder
   pinch of garlic granules**

Fold this into the crumbled tofu, and mix gently until coated.

Heat a lightly-oiled or non-stick skillet over high heat. Pour in the tofu and scrape and turn the mixture with a flat spatula until the tofu has turned a nice, scrambled egg-yellow, is hot through, and is as creamy or dry as you like it. Serve hot with salt and pepper (and ketchup, if you like!). You can sprinkle the tofu with soy bacon bits and/or minced parsley or other fresh herbs, if desired.

Per serving: Calories: 76, Protein: 12 gm., Carbohydrates: 5 gm., Fat: 1 gm.

VARIATION

Vegetable Scrambled Tofu

Make Scrambled Tofu as above. In another lightly oiled or non-stick, heavy skillet, steam-fry **½ cup sliced fresh mushrooms, ½ small sliced onion,** and **2 Tbsp. diced red or green bell pepper** over high heat until the onion and mushrooms begin to brown. Stir into the Scrambled Tofu, or pour the vegetables over it.

No-Oil Granola

Makes about 3 quarts.

A great nut substitute for use in baked goods.

In a large bowl or pot, combine thoroughly:

8 cups rolled oats or other flaked hot cereal (or a mixture)

3 cups whole wheat flour (or other whole grain flour or meal)

2 cups of one or a mixture of the following: wheat germ, wheat or other bran, soy grits, millet, okara (soy pulp leftover from making soymilk or tofu)

1 cup honey plus 1 cup hot water,
   or 1½ cups other liquid sweetener + ½ cup hot water

1 tsp. salt

1 tsp. vanilla

1 to 2 tsp. coconut or other nut extract (opt.)

Mix well, stirring for about 1 minute to make sure that everything is coated. Preheat the oven to 250°F. Spread the mixture on 2 large, lightly-oiled or non-stick cookie sheets with sides. Bake for 20 minutes, then stir the mixture every 5 minutes for the next 20 to 40 minutes to prevent burning. The total baking time will be 40 to 60 minutes, and the granola should be ready when it is lightly browned. (You can bake a double batch of this granola in a roasting pan at 200°F for about 3 hours, stirring every 30 minutes.)

Cool the granola thoroughly in the pans, and store in tightly sealed plastic bags, or other containers. I freeze it to have on hand for baking and add it straight to recipes from the freezer.

Per ½ cup: Calories: 231, Protein: 9 gm., Carbohydrates: 43 gm., Fat: 3 gm.

Drop Scones or Biscuits

Makes 14 to 16 scones or biscuits

This adaptation of an old British recipe proves that you don't need a lot of fat to make a light and tender biscuit or scone. Moist dough and light handling ensure that they will not be tough or dry. Eat them hot if possible, but they can be successfully re-heated.

Preheat oven to 400°F.

Mix together in a medium bowl:

> **2 cups flour (half unbleached white flour and/or half whole wheat pastry flour)**
> **½ tsp. baking soda**
> **½ tsp. salt**
> **1 tsp. sugar**
> **1 tsp. baking powder**

If you like, you can add minced parsley to the basic mixture, experiment with various dried fruits (like apricots and prunes) and spices (like cardamom), add grated citrus peel for flavor, and use the dough for cobblers and pandowdy. For herbal biscuits, add ¼ tsp. pepper, ½ tsp. minced garlic, 1 Tbsp. minced fresh basil, 2 Tbsp. minced fresh chives, and 1 tsp. minced fresh oregano, thyme, or marjoram.

Stir in with a fork:

> **1¼ cups reduced-fat soymik mixed with 1 Tbsp. lemon juice**

Stir quickly to moisten the dry ingredients. Drop the mixture by large spoonfuls onto lightly greased or non-stick cookie sheets, far enough apart so they don't touch. Smooth the tops a bit with wet fingers, and sprinkle with sugar, caraway seeds, sesame seeds, or poppy seeds, if you like.

Bake in a 400°F oven for about 10 minutes, or until golden brown on the bottom and beginning to color on the top. Serve immediately, if possible.

Per scone: Calories: 62, Protein: 2 gm., Carbohydrates: 12 gm., Fat: 0 gm.

Featherlight Dumplings

Makes about 8 dumplings

If you like, add some fresh chopped parsley or other herbs to the dough.

Mix in a medium bowl:

1 cup unbleached flour
2 tsp. baking powder
¼ tsp. salt

Stir in to make a stiff dough:

½ cup reduced-fat soymilk

Stir briefly just to mix. Drop small spoonfuls of dough on top of simmering stew or soup, cover tightly, and cook without lifting the lid for 10 minutes. Test one dumpling to see if it's done in the middle before serving.

Per dumpling: Calories: 57, Protein: 2 gm., Carbohydrates: 12 gm., Fat: 0 gm.

Basic Light and Easy Muffins

Makes 12 muffins

These muffins are light, tender, and perfectly-risen, thanks to the same tofu-liquid mixture in the cake recipes in the dessert chapter.

Preheat the oven to 350°F.

In a medium bowl, mix together:

> 1¼ cup unbleached white or whole wheat pastry flour
> ⅓ cup oat flour (see pg. 19)
> 1 tsp. baking powder
> 1 tsp. baking soda
> ½ -1 tsp. salt
> ½ -1 cup dried fruit, chopped,
>   or 1 cup fresh fruit, chopped and well-drained,
>   or berries (opt.)
> ½ tsp. cinnamon (opt.)
> ½ tsp. nutmeg (opt.)

In a blender, mix until very smooth:

> 8 oz. reduced-fat, medium-firm regular tofu
> ¼ -½ cup sugar,* honey, or Sucanat®
> ½ cup water or fruit juice (if you are adding very juicy fruit, use only ⅓ cup)
> 1 Tbsp. lemon juice
> 1-2 Tbsp. nutritional yeast flakes (opt.)
> 1 Tbsp. molasses (opt.)
> 1-3 Tbsp. vanilla or other flavor extract, or grated citrus zest

*If you prefer not to use sugar, replace the sugar or honey, lemon juice, and water with **1 (6 oz.) can thawed, frozen apple juice concentrate (¾ cup) plus 1 Tbsp. water.** You can omit this extra water if you are adding very juicy fruit.

Pour the blended mixture into the flour mixture, and stir just until all of the dry ingredients are well-moistened. Spoon the batter evenly into 12 lightly greased or non-stick muffin cups. Bake for 20 minutes. If the muffins are too crusty for your taste, loosen them and turn them on their sides in the pan, then cover with a clean tea towel for 5 minutes while still hot from the oven.

Paper muffin cups stick to very low-fat mixtures, so it's better not to use them.

Serve with *Corn Butter*, pg. 46, and/or jam. These freeze and reheat well.

Per muffin: Calories: 96, Protein: 4 gm., Carbohydrates: 19 gm., Fat: 0 gm.

Blueberry Muffins

VARIATIONS

Mix **1 cup fresh or well-drained, thawed, frozen blueberries** with 2 Tbsp. of the flour mixture, then fold into the batter after the dry and liquid ingredients are combined.

Orange-Cranberry Muffins

Use **orange juice** for the liquid, and add **1 Tbsp. orange zest** and **1 cup chopped cranberries.**

Orange-Coconut Muffins

Same as above, but omit cranberries and add ½ cup *No-Oil Granola* (pg. 79). Use **1 tsp. coconut extract.**

Lemon-Poppy Seed Muffins

For the liquid, use **4 Tbsp. lemon juice** and **5 Tbsp. water.** Use **nutmeg (opt.)** and **yeast flakes**, and **½ cup sugar.** Use **1 Tbsp. lemon extract** or **grated zest of ½ a lemon** and add **2 Tbsp. poppy seeds.**

Bran Muffins

Makes 12 muffins

Paper muffin cups stick to very low-fat mixtures, so it's better not to use them.

Preheat oven to 350°F.

In a medium bowl, mix together:

> **2 cups reduced-fat soymilk**
> **1½ cups wheat bran**
> **¾ cup raisins, currants, or chopped dates (opt.)**
> **½ cup light or dark molasses**
> **½ tsp. salt**
> **¼ cup sugar or Sucanat® (opt.)**

In a larger bowl, mix:

> **2 cups flour (unbleached white and/or whole wheat pastry)**
> **1 tsp. baking soda**
> **1 tsp. baking powder**
> **2 tsp. cinnamon (opt.)**

Pour the milk and bran mixture into the flour mixture, and combine briefly, just until moistened. Spoon evenly into 12 non-stick or lightly-greased muffin cups. Bake for 20 minutes. Cool on a rack covered with a clean towel.

Per muffin: Calories: 180, Protein: 4 gm. Carbohydrates: 40 gm., Fat: 1 gm.

VARIATION   ## Ready-Bake Bran Muffins

You can double or triple this batter, and keep it in a covered jar or rigid plastic container in your refrigerator for a week or two, to make muffins as you need them. Stir the batter gently before using.

Light and Easy Corn Muffins

Makes 12 muffins

Preheat the oven to 350°F.

In a blender, mix until very smooth:

> **8 oz. reduced-fat, firm or medium-firm regular tofu**
> **½ cup water**
> **⅓ cup sugar or Sucanat®,**
>   **or ¼ cup honey***
> **2 Tbsp. nutritional yeast flakes**
> **1 Tbsp. lemon juice**

In a medium bowl, mix together:

> **⅞ cup unbleached white flour**
> **¾ cup cornmeal**
> **1 tsp. baking soda**
> **1 tsp. baking powder**
> **1 tsp. salt**

*If you prefer not to use sugar, replace the sugar or honey, water, and lemon juice with **½ cup thawed, frozen apple juice concentrate plus 3 Tbsp. water.**

These corn muffins are light and tender, with plenty of corn flavor. This is definitely "Yankee" corn bread—on the sweet side. You can adjust the sugar to taste.

Paper muffin cups stick to very low-fat mixtures, so it's better not to use them.

Pour the blended mixture into the dry mixture, and mix just until the dry ingredients are moistened. Spoon into 12 greased or non-stick muffin cups. Bake 20 minutes. If you like a softer crust on your muffins, loosen them, turn them on their sides, and cover with a clean tea towel for 5 minutes while still hot from the oven.

For extra flavor, you can add 1 tsp. cumin seeds, ½ cup steam-fried onions, 1 cup corn kernels, ¼ cup chopped green chilies, or 2 Tbsp. soy bacon bits.

Per muffin: Calories: 103, Protein: 4 gm Carbohydrates: 20 gm., Fat: 0 gm.

Flour Tortillas

Makes 8 to 12

Commercial corn tortillas contain no added fat, but the flour ones usually do—and it's often lard or hydrogenated shortening. If you like flour tortillas for burritos and quesadillas, try this easy recipe for making your own.

In a medium bowl, mix:
3 cups flour (unbleached white, or part whole wheat pastry flour)
2 tsp. baking powder
¾ tsp. salt

Add and knead briefly on a floured surface:
1 cup warm water

When the dough is smooth, place it in a greased bowl, cover with plastic or a wet cloth, and let "rest" for 15 minutes at least, but preferably several hours.

Cut the dough into 8 to 12 equal-sized pieces, and form into balls. On a well-floured surface, roll the balls out to very thin circles, as round as you can manage.

Heat a large skillet or griddle (a cast iron frying pan works well) over high heat until it is very hot. Carefully place one tortilla in the pan, and cook until the edges start to look dry and there are brown flecks on the bottom. Flip the tortilla over and cook the other side; it takes only a few moments. It's okay if there are some dark spots, but the tortilla should be flexible and not brown all over.

Repeat with the remaining tortillas, and stack them up on a plate as you cook, covering them with a clean towel. Serve immediately or let cool.

You can store the cool tortillas wrapped in foil or inside of a plastic bag, and refrigerate or freeze them. Reheat the thawed tortillas in the foil in a 350°F oven for about 15 minutes. You can keep the tortillas hot and soft for as long as 2 hours by wrapping the hot foil package in a towel, then in several layers of newspaper.

Per tortilla: Calories: 121, Protein: 4 gm., Carbohydrates: 26 gm., Fat: 0 gm.

Fat-Free Sweet Yeast Bread Dough

Makes 2 loaves or 32 rolls

In a large mixing bowl, mix:

> **2 cups warm water**
> **1 pkg. baking yeast**

When yeast is dissolved, add:

> **1 cup leftover mashed potatoes (½ lb. russet pota-**
> **toes, cooked and mashed),**
> **or 1 cup instant mashed potato flakes mixed**
> **with ⅔ cup boiling water**
> **½ cup wheat germ**
> **¼ cup soymilk powder**
> **¼ cup honey**
> **¼ cup sugar**
> **1 Tbsp. lemon juice**
> **2 tsp. salt**
> **¼ tsp. turmeric**

I love to bake yeast breads, and this dough works well for many recipes that call for doughs rich with eggs and butter. Please do experiment by adapting your favorite sweet, rich bread dough recipes (such as special Christmas or Easter breads) for use with this dough. By adding extra honey, yeast, and a bit of turmeric for color, this dough makes tender sweet breads and challah.

Mix in:

> **5 cups unbleached flour**

Knead well for 5-10 minutes, using as little flour as possible (this dough should be soft and a bit sticky).

Place in a greased bowl, and rise overnight in the refrigerator (this dough handles best when cold). If you wish, you can let it rise until doubled either once or twice. Shape into two loaves or 32 small rolls. Cover and rise until doubled. Bake at 350°F for 45 minutes for the loaves, 20-25 minutes for rolls.

Per roll: Calories: 90, Protein: 3 gm., Carbohydrates: 19 gm., Fat: 0 gm.

Challah

Divide the risen *Fat-Free Sweet Yeast Bread Dough* equally in half. Make 2 braided loaves. Just before baking, brush with *Starch Glaze* and sprinkle with **sesame or poppy seeds**. Bake as for loaves in the basic recipe.

Fat-Free Cinnamon Sticky Buns

Divide the risen *Fat-Free Sweet Yeast Bread Dough* equally in half. Roll each half into a 12" x 18" rectangle. Spread each rectangle with **2 Tbsp. Corn Butter** (pg. 46), or **Tofu Sour Cream** (pg. 37), and sprinkle with **1½ tsp. cinnamon, and ½ cup raisins or currants.** Roll up lengthwise and seal the long edge well. Cut each roll into 1" slices with a sharp knife. Place the slices cut-side-down in two 9" x 13" baking pans in which you have spread **½ cup maple syrup or other syrup,** or **⅓ cup honey plus 1 Tbsp. water and 1 Tbsp. molasses.** Let rise until doubled, then bake at 350°F for 20 to 25 minutes. Invert on a cookie sheets to cool.

Savory Hamburger Rolls

Make the *Fat-Free Sweet Yeast Bread Dough,* but use only half a packet of yeast. Omit the sugar and honey, or use only 2 Tbsp. honey. The turmeric is optional. Omit the wheat germ and add **1 cup whole wheat flour.** You can add herbs to this recipe or use it for filled breads like calzone, etc.

Starch Glaze

Use this in place of egg white to help toppings adhere to the tops of loaves or for a shiny crust. Mix **½ cup cold water** with **1 tsp. cornstarch** in a small saucepan. Stir and cook over high heat until thickened and clear.

Bright Ideas . . .

Filled Breads

In my opinion, there is nothing more satisfying than savory, filled buns. It's pretty hard to feel deprived when feasting on these treats. And they make great lunch box fare too.

Use either the *Yeast Dough*, pg. 81, or your own favorite, fat-free dough, risen once and rolled thinly to the size you want (some people like two-bite rolls, others like big ones). You can make rounds, ovals, or squares. Fill (not too full) with any of these suggestions, or whatever else sounds good to you: fat-free, vegetarian stews, chiles, bean dishes, sloppy joe filling, vegetarian loaves or pâté, steam-fried mushrooms and other vegetable mixtures (alone, or bound with *Golden* or *Tangy Cream Sauce*, pg. 41, or *Tofu Sour Cream*, pg. 37, pizza toppings, sauerkraut and chopped "*Sausage*," pg. 27, or tofu wieners, chopped barbecued seitan or tofu, or textured vegetable protein with barbecue sauce to moisten, slices of tomato, bell pepper, roasted eggplant, steam-fried mushrooms and onions, or fresh basil with a bit of *Tangy Cream Sauce*, pg. 41.

Bring the dough up around the filling, and pinch the edges together to seal. Place the breads at least one inch apart on greased or non-stick cookie sheets, brush with reduced-fat soymilk, and bake in a preheated 400°F oven for 10 to 15 minutes, (until golden). Serve hot or at room temperature; you can freeze these if the filling is freezable.

Filled Bread Squares

This is easier to make than *Filled Breads*, but messier to eat. Use a thick filling. Instead of making little separate buns, roll the dough out thinly, and line a greased or non-stick cookie sheet with sides, overlapping the sides a bit with dough. Spread the filling on evenly to the top of the pan sides. Top with another sheet of thinly-rolled dough, and seal the edges all around. Prick the top all over with a fork, and bake as above. When cool, cut into squares.

Chapter 4
Soups, Salads & Dressings

My mother and my grandmother both made pots of thick, hearty soup for dinner at least once a week—and that *was* dinner (along with some crusty bread and salad), not just the first course! Soup is still a perfect meal for me any time of day, even soup for breakfast. It was hard to choose just a few, good soup recipes to include in this collection, because there are so many delicious ones, and soup is so easy to adapt to no-fat-added cooking. I've concentrated on meal-in-a-bowl soups, because I like them better than thin, first-course soups. You can easily adapt your favorite soup recipes by substituting vegetarian stocks for meat stocks, by steam-frying onions and other vegetables, by using herbs, onion, garlic, soy sauce, nutritional yeast, and wine for rich flavor, and by thickening cream soups with *Plain Rice Milk*, pg. 40, or *Tofu Sour Cream*, pg. 37, instead of cream and sour cream.

It's wonderful to make your own soup stocks, but many of us don't seem to find the time for it anymore. I've included a few ideas for vegetarian stock (it's much quicker to make than meat stock), but you can use a commercial vegetarian stock if you wish. Try out all of the vegetarian cubes, powders, and bouillon bases that are available to you, and keep your favorite on hand. When you make stock, freeze it in the quantities that you use most often.

When you cook garbanzo beans or soybeans, save the broth and freeze it; these beans make a very flavorful stock. The traditional, Chinese vegetarian stock is made by simmering soybean sprouts and dried mushrooms (always save mushroom soaking water for use as a stock). Bean or mushroom broth with a bit of soy sauce and/or yeast extract (Marmite, Sovex, or Vegex) added is a good substitute for beef broth.

BASIC VEGETABLE STOCK

If you use organically-grown vegetables, you can save washed peelings, skins, trimmings, and scraps from your vegetables to make stock. Otherwise, wash and peel the vegetables before using in stock. If you do save trimmings, keep adding to a bag in the freezer until you have enough to make a potful (if you use a lot of vegetables, just keep a bag in the refrigerator for a few days). Home-dehydrated vegetables can be used too.

Fill your stock pot loosely with vegetables and/or trimmings. Cover them with water, adding herbs if desired. Cover and bring to a boil. Lower the heat and simmer for 1 to 2 hours. Strain the stock and discard the vegetables, then taste and adjust the seasoning.

For richer flavor, first steam-fry some of the vegetables (onions, celery, garlic, carrots) until browned before adding to the stock pot.

I usually avoid cabbage family vegetables from the soup stock because of their strong flavor, but use them if you like.

Stock Pot Vegetables :

onions (the skins add color too), green onions, and leeks
carrots (tops and skins of organic ones can be used)
celery (be sure to use the leaves too)
garlic (add at least a whole head to the pot, the flavor mellows
      as it cooks)
parsley (stems too, and you can use old-fashioned parsley root)
mushrooms (fresh or dried)
lettuce (wilted leaves are fine)
soybean sprouts
parsnips (these add a sweet flavor)
potatoes and potato peels (organic with no green spots)
zucchini and other summer squash
winter squash

Seasonings:
herbs and spices of your choice
nutritional yeast (adds a cheesy or chicken-style flavor)
wine
miso, soy sauce, and/or yeast extract (such as Marmite, Sovex,
     Vegemite, or Vegex) add a beefy flavor
salt to taste
pepper if you like it
vegetable bouillon cubes, base, or powder (if the stock
     seems a bit lacking in flavor)

Thick Onion Soup
Serves 6

This is a very satisfying, simple winter soup.

In a large, heavy pot, steam-fry until golden and soft:

    6 large onions, thinly sliced

Stir in:

    ¼ cup flour
    1 tsp. EACH paprika and salt

Blend well and add:

    2 cups water

Cover and simmer for 30 minutes. Meanwhile, boil in enough water to almost cover until tender:

    4 large potatoes, peeled and sliced

Mash the potatoes coarsely in whatever cooking water is left. Add the potatoes to the onion mixture with:

    2 cups reduced-fat soymilk,
      or Plain Rice Milk, pg. 40

Add salt and pepper to taste. Heat gently and sprinkle each serving with paprika and/or chopped parsley.

Per serving: Calories: 178, Protein: 4 gm., Carbohydrates: 38 gm., Fat: 1 gm.

"From the Hearth" Soup

Serves 8

This is versatile, delicious, and filling, and has never failed to please my guests.

In a large pot, steam-fry until soft:
    1 large onion, chopped

Add:

    8 cups vegetarian broth
    4-5 cups vegetables, chopped, sliced, or shredded
        (carrots, cabbage, and celery are good choices)
    ½ -1 cup cooked soybeans,
        or ⅓ cup soy grits
    1 cup canned tomatoes,
        2 cups fresh tomatoes,
        2 cups juice from canned tomatoes,
        or ½ (6 oz.) can of tomato paste mixed with 1
        cup water
    ½ cup uncooked brown rice
    ⅓ cup uncooked bulgur wheat
    2 Tbsp. soy sauce
    ¼ tsp. EACH dried basil, oregano, tarragon, celery
        seed, savory, thyme, rosemary, marjoram, sage
    pepper to taste
    a pinch of cayenne

Bring to a boil, then reduce the heat, cover, and simmer, one to two hours. If you wish, frozen corn, frozen peas, and fresh, chopped parsley can be added toward the end of cooking time.

Per serving: Calories: 137, Protein: 5 gm., Carbohydrates: 25 gm., Fat: 1 gm.

Golden Vegetable Noodle Soup

Serves 6

This soup has the same comforting effect as chicken noodle. My son loves this on a winter afternoon.

In a large pot, steam-fry until tender:

1 large onion, chopped
½ cup celery (stalks and leaves), chopped
1 clove garlic, minced

Add and simmer for 1 hour:

8 cups hot water
½ cup yellow split peas, rinsed
½ tsp. turmeric
1 bay leaf

Add:

1 cup broken, thin whole wheat or soy pasta
1 cup frozen peas
½ cup carrots, chopped
½ cup fresh parsley, chopped
⅓ cup nutritional yeast flakes
1 Tbsp. salt
½ Tbsp. soy sauce

Cook just until the noodles are soft and the carrots are tender, adding pepper if you like. If you're fighting a cold, a dash of cayenne in this soup is just what the doctor ordered!

Per serving: Calories: 159, Protein: 9 gm., Carbohydrates: 29 gm., Fat: 0 gm.

Thick and Creamy Split Pea Soup

Serves 8

This is good with corn bread or muffins. Sprinkle each serving with soy bacon bits, if you like, or add slices of tofu wieners.

Bring to a boil in a large pot:

10 cups vegetarian broth
1 lb. green or yellow split peas, rinsed
3-6 carrots, chopped
1 onion, chopped
1 cup celery (stalks and leaves), chopped
1-2 cloves garlic, minced
½ tsp. dried thyme
dash cayenne

If you like a really thick soup, add ¼ cup pearl or pot barley to the soup along with the peas. Turn the heat down, cover, and simmer for 2 to 4 hours, or until the peas are tender. If the soup is too thick, add some water. Taste for seasoning and add:

¼ cup fresh parsley, chopped
pepper to taste
a few drops of liquid smoke (opt.)

Per serving: Calories: 96, Protein: 5 gm., Carbohydrates: 19 gm., Fat: 0 gm.

Corn Chowder

Serves 6 to 8

You can use white beans or black-eyed peas or any other beans if you don't have kidneys or small reds, but the red beans are attractive in this soup. The beans can also be omitted, if you like.

Bring to a boil in a large pot:

> **3 cups vegetarian broth**
> **2 cups potatoes, peeled and diced**
> **1 small onion, chopped**
> **½ cup celery, chopped**
> **½ cup red bell pepper, chopped, (opt.)**
> **½ cup green bell pepper, chopped, (opt.)**
> **½ tsp. dried thyme**

Reduce heat, cover, and simmer until the potatoes are tender.

Add:

> **2½ cups reduced-fat soymilk or Plain Rice Milk, pg. 40, mixed with 2 Tbsp. cornstarch**
> **2 cups cooked corn kernels (1-16 oz. can)**
> **2 cups cooked or canned small red beans or kidney beans, drained (1-16 oz. can)**
> **2 Tbsp. nutritional yeast flakes**
> **1 tsp. salt**
> **½ tsp. ground cumin (opt.)**
> **pepper to taste**
> **pinch of cayenne**

Simmer on low heat until the soup thickens, stirring occasionally. Taste for seasoning, sprinkle on some black pepper or some chopped fresh parsley, and enjoy!

Per serving: Calories: 185, Protein: 8 gm., Carbohydrates: 37 gm., Fat: 1 gm.

Cream of Tomato Soup

Serves 6-8

A real treat when you have fresh tomatoes from the garden!

In a large heavy pot, steam-fry:
1 medium onion, chopped
1 carrot, chopped

When the onion is wilted, add:
3 lbs. ripe tomatoes, stemmed and cut into chunks,
or 2 (28 oz.) cans whole or diced tomatoes,
with their juice
1 tsp. fresh garlic, minced
1 tsp. salt

Simmer for 15 minutes, stirring occasionally. Puree the mixture in two batches in the blender. (You can sieve out the seeds, if you like.) Return to the pot and add:
2 Tbsp. vegetarian broth powder
1-2 Tbsp. tomato paste (depending on the intensity of the tomato flavor)
1-2 Tbsp. sugar
(depending on the acidity of the tomatoes)
1 bay leaf
1 tsp. dried dillweed,
or 1 Tbsp. fresh dillweed, chopped

Cover and simmer for 15 to 20 minutes more. Over low heat, stir in:
2 cups Plain Rice Milk, pg. 40, mixed with 2 Tbsp. cornstarch
1 cup cooked brown rice (opt.)

Taste for salt and pepper, and heat gently. Sprinkle each serving with dill, and serve the soup with *Tofu Sour Cream*, pg. 37, to spoon on top.

Per serving: Calories: 83, Protein: 2 gm., Carbohydrates: 17 gm., Fat: 0 gm.

Salads and Dressings

I grew up with an enormous salad bowl on the table almost every night of my life. Sometimes (especially in the summer) all we had for dinner was a huge green salad with some protein added (usually canned tuna) and big, home-made garlic croutons made from stale sourdough French bread. My mother's dressing was simply fresh lemon juice, olive oil, and salt, with fresh garlic ground to a paste.

To this day I find that most people are stingy with the salad—what I consider a serving for one or two has to do for six on many tables! A big, fresh green salad with an oil-free dressing will fill you up and do wonders for your digestion.

I'm telling you this because I don't want you to think that salads are unimportant to me, judging by the number of recipes in this section. It's just that I don't follow recipes for salads very often—I just use what I have around. In the summer, we use all varieties of crispy lettuce (everything but iceberg, which I don't find very tasty) with ripe tomatoes, cucumbers, bell peppers, and fresh herbs. As the weather grows colder, the lettuce gives way to more cabbage, broccoli, and cauliflower, often with grated carrots, beets, and turnips, home-grown sprouts, mushrooms, and canned artichoke hearts (a favorite of mine). In the dead of winter, our salad is basically a coleslaw of cabbage and carrots.

You can add any of your favorite vegetables to a salad (raw or lightly steamed)— for instance, sliced or slivered summer squash, green onions, red onions, green beans, ji-cama, fresh water chestnuts or Jerusalem artichokes (for crunch), celery, cress, or anything else you can think of. Fruit also can be added. For a heartier salad, add croutons, roasted soybeans or garbanzo beans, cooked or canned beans, sliced, baked marinated tofu of any kind (pages 22-24), slivers of seitan, sliced, vegetarian deli "meats," or cooked potato. You are limited only by your taste and imagination.

There are many oil-free commercial dressings available today, but I always make my own. I find them fresher, cheaper, and more delicious, but if you have found some oil-free varieties that you enjoy, by all means use them. If you like just fresh lemon juice or vinegar on your greens, perhaps with a sprinkle of salt and herbs, that's great. But if you like the dressing to stick to the leaves, try my easy *Oil Substitute for Salad Dressing*, pg. 98, substituting it measure-for-measure for oil in any of your favorite salad dressing recipes.

Salad dressing is a very individual thing—some people like more vinegar, others more salt or garlic. Feel free to change proportions and seasonings in my recipes to suit your own taste.

Bright Idea . . .

For Crisp Lettuce

As soon as you pick the lettuce or bring it home, separate the leaves, discarding any bad ones, and soak in cold water for 15 minutes. Dry the leaves by using a salad spinner or laying them on a large, clean towel, rolling the towel up loosely, holding the ends firmly and spinning the roll around. Remove the leaves, wrap them in moist towels, and place in a plastic bag (or in a special plastic salad storage container) in the refrigerator. Lettuce will keep fresh longer this way. This method can also be used for reviving wilted lettuce.

Low-Fat American Potato Salad

Serves 6

I've served this countless times to guests who came back for seconds and thirds, never suspecting this wasn't the fat-laden, eggy potato salad of their youth.

Cut into quarters:

> **2½ -3 lbs. red or white thin-skinned potatoes, un-peeled (about 6 medium)**

Boil in water to cover until just tender. Drain and peel under cold running water. Immediately slice or dice the potatoes however you like them. Place in a large bowl, and toss while still warm with:

> **2-3 Tbsp. brine from a jar of dill pickles**

Add to the potatoes:

> **1 recipe Tofu Mayonnaise, pg. 36**
> **⅔ cup dill pickle, chopped**
> **1 small onion, minced**
> **1 Tbsp. nutritional yeast flakes**
> **2 tsp. prepared Dijon-style mustard**
> **1 tsp. turmeric**
> **salt and pepper to taste**
> **½ cup celery, chopped (opt.)**
> **½ cup red or green bell pepper, chopped (opt.)**
> **fresh dillweed (opt.)**

If you have no dill pickle, use chopped cucumber or celery, and add salt, dillweed, and white wine vinegar to taste to replace the pickle brine above.

Moisten with more of the dill pickle brine, making the salad runnier than you want it to end up—the potatoes will soak up the dressing. Cover and chill until serving time.

Per serving: Calories: 199, Protein: 3 gm., Carbohydrates: 44 gm., Fat: 0 gm.

Caesar Salad

Serves 4

Because of the anchovies, cheese, eggs, and excessive oil in a classic Caesar, I thought it was a never-to-be-again memory—until I came up with this recipe.

Wash and trim:
1 large head of Romaine lettuce

Dry thoroughly and place in a plastic bag or container in the refrigerator to crisp.

Make a dressing by mixing together in a small saucepan:
1 cup water
1½ Tbsp. cornstarch

Stir over high heat until it is clear and thick. Place in a blender with:
6 Tbsp. fresh lemon juice
3 Tbsp. light or white miso
1 Tbsp. nutritional yeast flakes
2 large cloves garlic, peeled
½ tsp. kelp powder (opt.)
¼ tsp. dry mustard
1 tsp. Vegetarian Worcestershire Sauce, pg. 48 (opt.)

Blend well, then place in a shallow bowl. Chill in the refrigerator (or even in the freezer, if you're in a hurry). To make garlic croutons, preheat the oven to 300° F, and toast on a cookie sheet until golden:
6 slices French, Italian, or sourdough French bread

Rub the toast on both sides with:
3 large cloves garlic, peeled

Cut the toast into ½" cubes. Set aside.

Just before serving, tear the lettuce coarsely in a salad bowl, and toss with half of the cold dressing. Add:
the garlic croutons
½ cup Soy Cheesy Gomasio, pg. 37, or soy Parmesan
lots of freshly ground black pepper

Toss well and serve immediately. Refrigerate the remaining dressing in a covered bottle in the refrigerator for up to 2 weeks.

Per serving: Calories: 199, Protein: 11 gm., Carbohydrates: 29 gm., Fat: 3 gm.

Garlic Slaw

Serves 8

This will wake up a sleepy winter palate!

Combine in a blender until very smooth:

    ⅞ cup reduced-fat soymilk
    ⅓ cup cider vinegar
    ¼ cup honey
    ¼ cup reduced-fat, firm silken or medium-firm regular tofu
    4 large cloves garlic, peeled
    1 tsp. salt

In a large bowl, toss this dressing with:

    8 cups green cabbage, finely shredded or chopped, or a mixture of cabbage and carrots

Cover the bowl tightly with plastic wrap, and refrigerate until serving time.

Per serving: Calories: 69, Protein: 1 gm., Carbohydrates: 14 gm., Fat: 0 gm.

Oil Substitute for Salad Dressing

Makes 1 cup

Use this in place of the oil in your favorite dressings; (it will thicken further when chilled).

Mix together in a small saucepan:

1 cup cold water or light vegetarian broth
2 tsp. cornstarch

Cook, stirring constantly, over high heat until thickened and clear.

Per Tbsp.: Calories: 1, Protein: 0 gm., Carbohydrates: 0 gm., Fat: 0 gm.

Oil-Free Italian Dressing

Makes about 1⅓ cups

Mix together in a covered jar:

1 cup Oil Substitute for Salad Dressings, pg. 98
¼ cup red wine vinegar
1 Tbsp. Dijon-style prepared mustard
½ Tbsp. honey
1-2 cloves of garlic, crushed
1 tsp. salt or herbal salt
1 tsp. dried basil
¼ tsp. paprika
pepper to taste

Per 2 Tbsp.: Calories: 16, Protein: 0 gm., Carbohydrates: 3 gm., Fat: 0 gm.

Sweet and Sour Dressing

Makes about 2 cups

If you like a sweet dressing, perhaps for a spinach salad, try this one. It's also great on bean salad.

Combine in a blender, then refrigerate in a covered jar:

1 cup Oil Substitute for Salad Dressings, pg. 98
⅔ cup red wine, cider, or rice vinegar
2 Tbsp. honey
3 cloves garlic, crushed
2 tsp. salt
1 tsp. soy sauce,
    or Vegetarian Worcestershire Sauce, pg. 48
1 tsp. freshly ground pepper
1 tsp. dry mustard

Per 2 Tbsp.: Calories: 13, Protein: 0 gm., Carbohydrates: 3 gm., Fat: 0 gm.

Bright Idea . . .

Easy Coleslaw Dressing

Simply mix *Tofu Mayonnaise*, pg. 36, with any kind of fruit juice until it is thin enough and sweet enough to your taste. You can flavor this with spices or herbs, if you wish.

Creamy Dill Dressing

Makes about 2 cups

Combine in the blender until very smooth:

> 1 (10.5 oz.) pkg. reduced-fat, extra-firm silken tofu,
>   or 8 oz. reduced-fat, firm or medium-firm regular
>   tofu
> ½ cup water
> ¼ cup lemon juice
> ¼ cup fresh parsley
> ¼ cup green onion
> 1 Tbsp. fresh dillweed, chopped,
>   or 1 tsp. dried dillweed
> 1 Tbsp. fresh basil,
>   or 1 tsp. dried basil
> ¾ tsp. salt
> ¼ tsp. sugar
> 1 clove garlic, crushed
> pinch cayenne

If the dressing is too thick, add a little more water. To make a thicker dill dip, use less water.

Per 2 Tbsp.: Calories: 8, Protein: 1 gm., Carbohydrates: 1 gm., Fat: 0 gm.

"Cheezy" Salad Dressing

Makes about 1½ cups

Combine in the blender until smooth:

> ½ (10.5 oz.) pkg. reduced-fat, extra-firm silken tofu,
> or ½ cup reduced-fat, firm or medium-firm
> regular tofu, crumbled
> ⅓ cup water
> 3 Tbsp. lemon juice
> 2 Tbsp. Sesame Meal, pg. 47
> 1 Tbsp. cider, white wine, or rice vinegar
> 1 tsp. salt,
> or 1 Tbsp. white miso + ½ tsp. salt
> 1 large clove garlic, crushed
> ¼ tsp. white pepper
> ¼ tsp. soy sauce or Vegetarian Worcestershire
> Sauce, pg. 48

If the mixture is too thick, add a little more water. Keep refrigerated in a covered jar.

Per 2 Tbsp.: Calories: 11, Protein: 1 gm., Carbohydrates: 1 gm., Fat: 0 gm.

Low-Fat Poppy Seed Dressing

This is delightful on fruit salads or Romaine lettuce and either orange or grapefruit sections. It's equally good on exotic fruits such as mango and papaya.

Makes about 1¾ cups

Shake together in a covered jar:

1 cup Oil Substitute for Salad Dressing, pg. 98
6 Tbsp. lemon juice
¼ cup honey
1 to 2 Tbsp. poppy seeds
½ tsp. salt
1 tsp. dry mustard
1 tsp. paprika
1 tsp. lemon zest, grated

Per 2 Tbsp.: Calories: 26, Protein: 0 gm., Carbohydrates: 6 gm., Fat: 0 gm.

Honey-Garlic-Mustard Dressing

This versatile dressing is good on greens or fruit salads.

Makes about 1⅓ cups

Mix in a blender:

1 cup Oil Substitute for Salad Dressings, pg. 98, made with broth
¼ cup cider vinegar
2 Tbsp. honey
2 Tbsp. Dijon-style prepared mustard
2 Tbsp. Tofu Mayonnaise, pg. 36
2-3 cloves garlic, crushed
½ tsp. salt
pepper to taste

Per 2 Tbsp.: Calories: 14, Protein: 0 gm., Carbohydrates: 3 gm., Fat: 0 gm.

Chapter 5

Oven-Baked Entrees

Most of the recipes in this chapter are perfect for company dinners or busy times. You can make them ahead of time, as they require little or no tending to while they cook. Often you can cook the whole dinner in the oven. For instance, try *Vegetarian Shepherd's Pie*, pg. 106, with baked squash, or *"Swiss Steak" Vegetarian-Style*, pg. 111, cooked with a variety of vegetables and baked potatoes on the side. Most of the other dishes require only a salad and rolls to round out the meal.

Eastern Baked Beans

Serves 6

I've always loved real, New England-style baked beans, with no new-fangled extras like tomato sauce. In this simple recipe, the roasted sesame meal stands in for the salt pork flavor; otherwise, the ingredients are few and simple. The results are lots of good eating!

Soak in water to cover for 8 hours:

2 cups small white navy or pea beans

Drain off the soaking water, and bring the soaked beans to a boil in a large pot with:

6 cups water

Lower the heat and simmer the beans for 10 minutes. Drain the beans and reserve the cooking water. Preheat the oven to 300°F. Place the beans in a casserole or bean pot, and mix with:

2 Tbsp. Sesame Meal, pg. 47

Insert into the center of the beans:

1 small onion, peeled and whole

Combine and pour over the beans, stirring well:

1 cup reserved bean liquid
¾ cup fancy molasses,
   or ½ cup honey or other liquid sweetener + ¼
      cup blackstrap molasses
2 tsp. salt
1 tsp. dry mustard

Add just enough reserved bean liquid to cover the beans. Cover the pot and bake for 2 hours. Add:

the remaining bean liquid

Stir well and bake for 1½ to 2 hours more, or until the beans are very tender and the liquid is absorbed. Bake uncovered for the last half hour.

Per serving: Calories: 372, Protein: 12 gm., Carbohydrates: 78 gm., Fat: 1 gm.

Savory Tofu Dinner Loaf

Serves 6

In a large bowl, mix:
> **1 cup fresh whole wheat bread crumbs**
> **⅓ cup water**

In a large, lightly oiled or non-stick skillet, steam-fry:
> **2 cups onion, minced (2 large onions)**
> **2 large cloves garlic, minced**

When the onions are very soft and beginning to brown, they are ready. This is very important to the taste and texture of the dish, so don't under-cook them. Add the onions to the bread crumbs along with:

> **1½ lbs. frozen reduced-fat, firm or medium-firm regular tofu, thawed, squeezed, and crumbled**
> **¼ cup soy sauce**
> **½ Tbsp. tomato paste or 1 Tbsp. ketchup**
> **½ tsp. EACH dried basil, sage, and oregano**
> **¼ tsp. dried thyme**
> **¼ tsp. dried savory**
> **1 tsp. Kitchen Bouquet® (opt., for color)**
> **pepper to taste**

Mix well and allow the mixture to cool (you can speed this up by placing it in the freezer for a few minutes). Preheat the oven to 350°F. When the mixture is cool, add:

> **¼ cup instant gluten flour (vital wheat gluten), or ⅓ cup whole wheat flour.**

Mix well and pat the mixture into a lightly-greased or non-stick, 9-inch round cake or pie pan. If you like, spread the top with a thin layer of ketchup. Bake for 30 minutes, then let sit for 10-15 minutes before cutting into wedges.

If you are craving good old American meat loaf, you are in for a treat. This simple recipe is amazingly good, either hot or cold, and makes delicious sandwiches. It can be doubled and you can try different seasonings according to your taste.

Per serving: Calories: 169, Protein: 19 gm., Carbohydrates: 15 gm., Fat: 4 gm.

Vegetarian Shepherd's Pie

Serves 6

Peel and quarter:

12 medium russet potatoes

Place in a large pot, and just cover with water. Bring to a boil, cover, and simmer until tender. Drain and keep warm.

While the potatoes are cooking, combine in a medium bowl:

1½ cups dry textured vegetable protein granules
1½ cups boiling water

Set aside to soak. (If you have no textured vegetable protein, use 2 cups frozen tofu, thawed, squeezed, and crumbled, or 2 cups ground seitan; omit the boiling water in either case.)

Simmer together for 10 minutes:

8 or 9 dried Chinese mushrooms
3 cups water

Drain (reserving the water), remove the stems, and chop the mushrooms. Set aside.

Have ready:

1 recipe Yeast Gravy, pg. 42, using the reserved mushroom cooking water for the liquid and omitting the salt

Simmer together in just enough water to cover until tender:

3 medium carrots, peeled and chopped
1 cup onions, chopped
¾ cup celery stalks and leaves, diced
1-2 cloves garlic, chopped

Drain. Preheat the oven to 400°F. In a shallow casserole dish, mix together:

> **the reconstituted textured vegetable protein**
> **the chopped mushrooms**
> **the cooked carrots, onions, celery, and garlic**
> **1½ cups frozen peas, thawed**
> **1 cup fresh or canned tomatoes, chopped**
> **2 Tbsp. soy sauce**
> **1 tsp. dried thyme**
> **½ tsp. crumbled sage**
> **½ tsp. dried marjoram**
> **½ tsp. ground pepper**

Add enough of the Yeast Gravy to moisten to your liking (save the rest to pass around at the table, adding a bit of salt if desired). Taste the casserole mixture and add salt and/or soy sauce if necessary.

Mash the drained potatoes and measure them; you should have about 7 cups. Add:

> **½ cup reduced-fat soymilk or other non-dairy milk**
> **1 tsp. salt**

Mash and whip the potatoes until they are fluffy, then spread them evenly over the casserole mixture. Sprinkle the top with:

> **1 Tbsp. Soy Cheesey Gomasio, pg. 37**
> **paprika**

Bake for 20 minutes or until bubbly.

Per serving: Calories: 453, Protein: 22 gm., Carbohydrates: 89 gm., Fat: 0 gm.

Lasagne

Serves 8

I love lasagne and it took me several years to come up with a meatless, cheeseless version that really pleased me. I've served this many times to confirmed meat-eaters, and there's never any leftovers.

Have ready:

1 recipe Tangy Cream Sauce, pg. 41

To make a lasagne sauce, steam-fry in a large, lightly oiled, heavy pot:

2 cups onion, minced
1 carrot, minced or grated
4 cloves garlic, minced

Combine in a small bowl:

1 cup dry textured vegetable protein granules
⅞ cup boiling water
1 Tbsp. soy sauce

Add to the pot with the vegetables:

the reconstituted textured vegetable protein
1 (28 oz.) can tomatoes and their juice, crushed
1 cup dry red wine or non-alcoholic wine
1 (6 oz.) can tomato paste
1 tsp. sugar
1 tsp. dried oregano
1 tsp. dried basil
pepper to taste

Simmer the mixture for about 20 minutes, then add to give a "meaty" taste:

soy sauce to taste

Set the sauce aside. In a large pot of boiling, salted water, boil until just tender:

18 lasagne noodles (about ¾ lb.)

Drain and set aside. Make a tofu filling by mixing together well:

> **2½ (10.5 oz.) pkgs. reduced-fat, extra-firm silken tofu,**
> **or 1½ lbs. reduced-fat, firm or medium-firm regular tofu, mashed**
> **1 (10 oz.) pkg. frozen chopped spinach, thawed and squeezed dry,**
> **or ½ cup fresh parsley, minced**
> **½-¾ cup reduced-fat soymilk or non-dairy milk**
> **1-2 tsp. salt**

To assemble the lasagne, use one lightly-oiled 9" x 13" pan or two 9" x 5" loaf pans. Preheat the oven to 350°F. Spread ¼ of the lasagne sauce on the bottom of the pan, then layer over 6 of the cooked noodles. Repeat with the same amount of sauce and then half of the tofu filling. Top with 6 more noodles and more sauce. Finish with the rest of the tofu filling, the remaining noodles, and the remaining sauce. Top with a thin layer of Tangy Cream Sauce and bread crumbs, if desired. Bake for 40 minutes and let stand for 10 minutes before serving. This reheats well if you want to make it ahead of time.

Per serving: Calories: 444, Protein: 26 gm., Carbohydrates: 72 gm., Fat: 4 gm.

Southern "Fried" Tofu

Serves 6

These crispy treats make a great party dish—kids and teenagers love them. They are also a great addition to a brown bag lunch.

Cut into 32 cubes:
1 lb. reduced-fat, firm or medium-firm regular tofu

Marinate for at least 12 hours in:
Breast of Tofu marinade, pg. 22

Have ready:
Seasoned Flour, pg. 49

Make up a dipping mixture by combining:
1 cup reduced-fat soymilk or non-dairy milk
1 Tbsp. nutritional yeast flakes
1 Tbsp. lemon juice
pinch salt
pinch onion powder
black pepper to taste

Preheat the oven to 400°F. Lightly oil two dark-colored cookie sheets. Remove the tofu cubes from the marinade, and coat with plain flour. Dip the floured cubes in the dipping mixture, coating all over, then roll them in the Seasoned Flour to coat. You may find this easiest if you use two separate forks for dipping the cubes in flour and two others for dipping in the liquid dipping mixture. Place the cubes, not touching, on the cookie sheets. Bake for 15 minutes, then turn the cubes over and bake 15 minutes more.

Serve the cubes hot with gravy (or equal parts ketchup and hot salsa) and mashed potatoes, or cold with the ketchup/salsa blend.

Per serving: Calories: 132, Protein: 12 gm., Carbohydrates: 16 gm., Fat: 1 gm.

Chile Chunks

VARIATION

These make a good appetizer. For the Seasoned Flour, substitute **¼ cup cornmeal** for ¼ cup of the flour, and add **2 tsp. chile powder, ¼ tsp. cumin, ¼ tsp. oregano** and **⅛ tsp. black pepper.** For a dipping sauce, flavor *Tofu Sour Cream*, pg. 37, with salsa to taste.

Bright Idea . . .

"Swiss Steak" Vegetarian-Style

Instead of steak, use your favorite vegetarian cutlet—such as seitan *Simmered Cutlets*, page. 30, or a commercial burger. Use one or two cutlets per serving. Layer the cutlets in a shallow baking pan. If you like, cover the cutlets with sliced and steam-fried onions, green peppers, mushrooms, carrots, etc.

Make an Espagnole sauce by mixing *Yeast Gravy*, page. 42, with an equal amount of vegetarian spaghetti or marinara sauce. Season with a bit of red wine if you like. Pour the sauce over the contents of the pan, cover, and bake at 350°F for 30 minutes. Serve with mashed potatoes, rice, or noodles. This is easy to make and quite delicious.

Tofu Pot Pie

Serves 6

This recipe, originally adapted from The Farm Vegetarian Cookbook (see pg. 192), has evolved over the last few years to this delicious and nearly fat-free version. It's a family favorite, especially for the holidays. For company occasions, you might prefer to use an ordinary pastry (preferably one of the lower-fat versions) or phyllo pastry with a little oil, but this recipe gives you several fat-free options that are very good.

Have ready and refrigerate one of the following:

½ recipe Yeasted Pastry, pg. 152
½ recipe Drop Scone Dough, pg. 74

Cut into ½" cubes:

1 lb. reduced-fat, firm or medium-firm regular tofu

Preheat the oven to 400°F. Mix in a paper bag:

½ cup whole wheat flour
1-2 Tbsp. nutritional yeast flakes
1 tsp. salt
½ tsp. garlic granules

Shake the tofu cubes in the paper bag until they are well-coated with the flour mixture. Place the cubes on a lightly-greased, dark-colored cookie sheet. Bake for 15 minutes, then turn the cubes over, and bake 15 minutes more, until they are golden and crispy. Set aside.

Prepare and set aside:

1 recipe Yeast Gravy, pg. 42, with only 1 Tbsp. soy sauce

To prepare the pot pie vegetables, lightly oil a large skillet. Steam-fry over high heat:

1 cup onion, chopped

When the onions have softened, add:

2 medium carrots, peeled and diced
4 oz. fresh mushrooms, sliced
½ cup celery, diced
¼ cup water

Cover the skillet and cook over medium-high heat for 10 minutes. Add:

> **1½ cups frozen peas**
> **2 Tbsp. soy sauce**
> **½ tsp. garlic granules**
> **the prepared tofu cubes**

Mix well and turn into a shallow, 10-inch casserole or a 10-inch deep dish pie pan. Pour in the Yeast Gravy, and mix well. Preheat the oven to 400°F.

Roll out whichever dough you are using—the Yeasted Pastry should be rolled out thinly like a pie dough; the biscuit doughs can be rolled out from ¼"-½" thick, depending on your preference. Cut the dough to fit the pan, then cover the tofu mixture with it. Cut slits in the top, and crimp the edges. If you like, brush the dough with soymilk, and sprinkle with sesame seeds.

Bake the pie for 30 minutes with a cookie sheet or pan underneath to catch any drips should the filling bubble over. Serve hot with mashed potatoes. This can also be made in small aluminum pie pans or casserole dishes for individual servings, which can be frozen before baking.

Per serving: Calories: 261, Protein: 18 gm., Carbohydrates: 41 gm., Fat: 2 gm.

Tamale Pie

Serves 6-8

Let's not kid our-selves—this is not a Mexican dish! I grew up in Califor-nia, so I consider it a Cal-Mex concoc-tion, but there are probably Tex-Mex and other versions. Some recipes con-tain beans and use a corn bread dough, but I prefer a ham-burger-like textured vegetable protein filling cov-ered with a cornmeal mush or polenta.

In a large, lightly-oiled pot, steam-fry:

2 cups onion, chopped
2 cloves garlic, minced

When the onions are soft and starting to brown, add and steam-fry for a few minutes:

2 Tbsp. chile powder
1 tsp. dried oregano
1 tsp. ground cumin

Add to the pan:

5½ cups water
2 cups dry textured vegetable protein granules
2 cups canned or frozen corn kernels, drained
2 large green peppers, seeded and chopped
2 (6 oz.) cans tomato paste
¼ cup soy sauce
2 Tbsp. sweetener of your choice
½ tsp. red pepper flakes (opt.)
salt and black pepper to taste

Let this mixture come to a boil, then turn the heat down, and simmer while you make a cornmeal topping.

In another large pot, mix together:

1½ cups cold water
1½ cups yellow cornmeal (not too finely ground)
1½ Tbsp. vegetable broth powder
1 tsp. salt

Add:

2½ cups boiling water

Stir over high heat with a long wooden spoon until it gets thick. Turn the heat to low, and cook for 5 minutes. Meanwhile, preheat the oven to 375°F.

Pour the filling into a 9" x 13" pan, and cover with the cornmeal topping. Smooth it out as well as you can, patching up any holes. If you wish, decorate the top with green or red bell pepper rings. Bake for 40 minutes. Reheat any leftovers by steaming.

Per serving: Calories: 307, Protein: 17 gm., Carbohydrates: 56 gm., Fat: 1 gm.

Golden Macaroni Casserole
Serves 2-4

Cook in a large pot of boiling, salted water until just tender:

5 oz. dry whole wheat or enriched macaroni, seashell pasta, penne, or rigatoni (1¼ cups uncooked)

Preheat the oven to 350°F. Drain the cooked macaroni and mix in a casserole with:

one recipe of Golden Sauce, pg. 41, using ½ cup nutritional yeast flakes
½ cup tomatoes, chopped and well drained, sautéed sliced onions, bell peppers, or mushrooms, or other steamed vegetables (opt.)

If desired, you can top the casserole with seasoned bread crumbs. Bake the casserole for 20 minutes. You can brown the top slightly under the broiler if you like.

If you're craving creamy macaroni and "cheese," look no further. This recipe is extremely easy to make, very low in fat, and very satisfying. This may seem very runny before you bake it, but the macaroni will soak up the sauce.

Per serving: Calories: 187, Protein: 12 gm., Carbohydrates: 29 gm., Fat: 1 gm.

Enchilada Casserole

Serves 6

This recipe is every bit as delicious as rolled enchiladas, but much easier, because there is no need to fry the tortillas and dip them in sauce. You can use your own favorite filling as a variation.

Make an enchilada sauce by steam-frying in a heavy skillet:

> **1½ cups onion, minced**

Mix together and add to the onions:

> **2 Tbsp. chile powder (ancho chile powder is good)**
> **2 Tbsp. flour**
> **¾ tsp. salt**
> **½ tsp. ground cumin**
> **¼ tsp. garlic granules**

Whisk in:

> **2 cups water**
> **3 Tbsp. tomato paste**

Bring to a boil, then turn down to low, cover, and simmer for 20 minutes. Salt to taste.

For the filling, steam-fry in a large, lightly oiled or non-stick heavy skillet:

> **1 large onion, thinly sliced**
> **1 large green or red bell pepper, seeded and sliced**
> **3-4 large cloves garlic, minced**
> **2 cups fresh mushrooms, sliced (opt.)**

When the onions have wilted, add:

> **2 cups frozen corn**
> **1½ tsp. ground cumin**
> **1½ tsp. dried oregano**
> **1½ tsp. chile powder**

Add salt to taste. Add:

> **2 cups canned or cooked pinto or black beans,**
> **or sliced seitan, Breast of Tofu, pg. 22, or Smoky**
> **Baked Tofu, pg. 24**

Other options to add to the filling instead of those above are crumbled frozen tofu, reconstituted textured vegetable protein granules flavored with soy sauce, textured vegetable protein chunks reconstituted in vegetable broth and sliced, or your favorite vegetarian burger, sliced or crumbled.

To assemble the casserole, have ready:

12 corn tortillas

Preheat the oven to 350°F. Spread a little bit of the enchilada sauce in the bottom of a 9" x 13" baking pan. Dip 4 of the tortillas into hot water, and layer them in the bottom of the pan, overlapping slightly. Top the tortillas with half of the filling. Dip 4 more tortillas into hot water, and layer them over the filling. Spread the rest of the filling on top, then dip the remaining 4 tortillas in hot water, and lay them on top. Pour the remaining enchilada sauce over this. If you wish, spread the top with a thin layer of *Tangy Cream Sauce or Golden Sauce*, pg. 41.

Cover the casserole with foil, and bake for 15 minutes. Remove the foil and bake 10-15 minutes more. Serve the casserole with *Tofu Sour Cream*, pg. 37, salsa, *Spanish Rice*, pg. 142, and a salad.

You can vary this recipe by using the tofu filling from the *Lasagne* recipe, pg. 108, and/or substituting your own favorite enchilada or molé sauce.

Per serving: Calories: 284, Protein: 10 gm., Carbohydrates: 55 gm., Fat: 2 gm.

Pizza

Don't think of pizza as a fatty junk food. Made with a fat-free, French or Italian-style bread crust (the way it should be), a fat-free tomato sauce, and any number of toppings (as bland or spicy as you like them), you can indulge to your heart's content. As for the question of cheese, be assured that not all authentic Italian pizzas contain cheese, and even when they do, Italians use less cheese than we are used to. If you like, drizzle the filled pizza with a thin stream of Tangy Cream Sauce, pg. 41. Depending on your dietary preferences, you can use a little grated soy Parmesan substitute. This pizza is so delicious, however, you may find you enjoy it without any

Makes two 14" round or 10" x 15" rectangular pizzas (16 pieces)

To make the pizza dough, dissolve and let stand for 10 minutes:

> **1 cup warm water**
> **1 tsp. baking yeast**

Add:

> **3 cups flour (can be ½ unbleached white and**
> **½ whole wheat)**
> **½ tsp. salt**

Stir well and add about 1 cup more flour as necessary, to make a kneadable dough. Knead on a floured surface for 5 minutes, then place in a lightly greased, medium bowl. Cover and let rise in a warm place for about 1½ -2 hours, or until doubled. You can easily make this dough in a food processor by adding the yeast and water to the flour and salt through the feed tube while the processor is running. Add enough flour so a ball of dough is formed on the blade; process for 30 seconds more.

For the pizza sauce, you can use your own favorite sauce, a commercial, fat-free brand, or make the following recipe. In a large, heavy, lightly oiled or non-stick skillet, steam-fry until softened:

> **½ cup onion, chopped**
> **2-3 cloves garlic, minced**

Add:

> **3 cups fresh or canned tomatoes, chopped**
> **1 (6 oz.) can tomato paste**
> **1 tsp. dried oregano**
> **1 tsp. dried basil**

Simmer and stir until the sauce is the consistency you desire, adding a bit of water if necessary. Add:

½ tsp. sweetener of your choice
salt and pepper to taste

When the dough has risen, punch it down and divide it in half. On a floured surface, roll each half out to fit a 14-inch round pizza pan or a 10" x 15" rectangular cookie sheet (dark pans make the best crusts). Fit the dough into the pans, and make a rim around the edge of each.

Preheat the oven to 450°F. Spread the sauce over the dough. Add any of the following pizza toppings:

any color of bell pepper, sliced, and steam-fried or
  raw
raw or steam-fried onion, sliced
fresh or steam-fried mushrooms, sliced
dried tomatoes, soaked and sliced
eggplant, roasted and sliced
artichoke hearts
fresh basil or other fresh herbs, chopped
garlic, chopped
Sesame Meal, pg. 47
Soy Cheesy Gomasio, pg. 37

Bake immediately for about 15 minutes, or until the bottom of the crust is golden and crispy. Cut each pizza into 8 slices. This can be reheated the next day (it freezes well too), and it's even good cold in a bag lunch.

cheese at all.
We generally do not use meat substitutes on pizza either, but if you prefer to, there are vegetarian pepperoni and sausage products on the market.

Per piece: Calories: 114, Protein: 4 gm., Carbohydrates: 22 gm., Fat: 1 gm.

Chapter 6
Top-of-the-Stove Entrees

In this section, beans play a major role. Low in fat, high in protein, fiber, and iron, cheap, versatile, filling, and satisfying—the list of beans' virtues is long. They deserve to come into their own in American cuisine.

Sometimes cooks are put off by the time it takes to pre-soak and cook beans. You can buy plain, canned beans in a pinch, but dried beans are much less expensive and leave no cans to dispose of. You don't always have to pre-soak beans, and you can make use of a very handy piece of cooking equipment: your pressure cooker. In a pressure cooker, you can cook some varieties of unsoaked beans in 30 minutes. Consult the bean cooking chart on pg. 186 for various methods of soaking and cooking.

Another staple in top-of-the-stove meals can be the stir-fry, but with a twist. Don't stir-fry in hot oil, but with a bit of water or broth instead. The technique is similar to steam-frying (see pg. 19). Have your vegetables cut ahead of time, and arrange them by length of cooking time. It's a good idea to blanch or partially cook less tender vegetables ahead of time, plunging them into ice cold water after draining, so they remain crisp and brightly colored. Lightly oil a large, heavy skillet or wok with about ½ teaspoon of oil (Chinese sesame oil is a nice choice for Asian dishes). Heat it over high heat. Add onions and garlic, if using, and a few dribbles of water. Stir-fry for a couple of minutes, then add the other vegetables, and stir-fry until they are crisp-tender. Add just enough liquid to keep them from sticking. Add your seasonings or cooking sauce, toss briefly, and serve.

Quick Marinara Sauce

Yield: 6-8 cups

In a large, heavy, lightly oiled or non-stick pot, steam-fry:

2 cups onions, minced
2-4 cloves of garlic, minced

When the onions are soft, add:

1 (28 oz.) can whole tomatoes and their juice
1 (6 oz.) can tomato paste
1 tsp. dried basil
1 tsp. dried oregano
1 bay leaf
½ tsp. sweetener of your choice
salt and pepper to taste

Optional additions to steam-fry along with the onions are:

fresh mushrooms, chopped or sliced
carrot, minced or grated
green pepper, chopped
fresh parsley and/or other fresh herbs, chopped
dried rosemary, marjoram, and/or sage
hot red pepper flakes

Crush the tomatoes with your fingers as you pour them into the pot. If the mixture is too thick, add some water or dry red wine. Bring to a boil, reduce the heat to low, cover, and simmer for about 20 minutes. Taste and adjust seasonings to your preference.

This will probably be a staple meal for many people, because spaghetti and tomato sauce is a satisfying dish. Vary it by using a different kind of pasta each time— rotelli, rigatoni, penne, linguine, etc. If you need a topping, try Soy Cheesy Gomasio, pg. 37.

Per cup: Calories: 58, Protein: 2 gm., Carbohydrates: 12 gm., Fat: 0 gm.

Old-Fashioned Vegetable Stew

Serves 6-8

Sure to become a family favorite, this stew lends itself to variation. Use whatever vegetables you have or prefer, wine or juice for some of the liquid, your own combination of herbs and spices, or add more tomato. Serve with rice, noodles, or bread instead of potatoes.

In a large, heavy, lightly oiled or non-stick pot, steam-fry:
2 medium onions, sliced
1 clove garlic, minced

When the onions are beginning to brown, add:
⅓ cup Browned Flour, pg. 49

Stir the flour around well, and then add:
5 cups water
½ cup dry red lentils
¼ cup soy sauce
¼ cup tomato paste
3-4 vegetable bouillon cubes
1 bay leaf
2 tsp. yeast extract, (opt., pg. 184)
1 tsp. sweetener of your choice
¼ tsp. dried thyme
¼ tsp. dried rosemary
¼ tsp. dried marjoram
black pepper to taste

Mix well and add:
4-5 cups cubed vegetables (mushroom halves, diced celery, diced eggplant, red or green bell pepper chunks, carrot, parsnip, rutabaga or turnip, peeled and chunked)
½ cup fresh parsley, chopped (opt.)
½ cup dry textured vegetable protein chunks, rehydrated, (opt.)
**2 cup seitan cubes, (opt.),
   or vegetarian burger (opt.)**

Simmer the stew for 30 minutes. Add:

1 cup frozen peas

Simmer 10 minutes more and taste for seasoning. Serve with steamed or mashed potatoes.

Per serving: Calories: 179, Protein: 12 gm., Carbohydrates: 31 gm., Fat: 0 gm.

Fat-Free Fried Rice

Serves 5-6

To make this dish properly, make sure the cooked rice is cold.

In a large, heavy, lightly oiled skillet or wok, steam-fry:

7-8 green onions, chopped
1 large stalk celery, minced
1 clove garlic, minced

After about 3 minutes, add and steam-fry:

1½ cups fresh mung bean sprouts
3-4 large, fresh mushrooms, sliced
¾ cup green cabbage, finely shredded

After about 2 minutes, add:

4½ cups cold, cooked brown rice

Lower the heat to medium, and steam-fry for 3-4 minutes. Add:

2½ Tbsp. soy sauce
black pepper to taste
1-2 Tbsp. Sesame Meal, pg. 47 (opt.)
1-2 Tbsp. vegetarian bacon bits (opt.)
1 cup Smoky Baked Tofu, cubed, pg. 24,
    or cooked seitan, slivered

Per serving: Calories: 233, Protein: 6 gm., Carbohydrates: 49 gm., Fat: 0 gm.

Best-Ever Tofu Burgers

Makes 6 large burgers

I've tried many vegetarian "burgers," and while many taste fine, I miss the chewy texture and juiciness associated with a truly good burger. Slices of frozen tofu provide the chewy-ness; this dark marinade lends a "meaty" flavor and moist juices. Serve these on fat-free rolls, pg. 82, with Tofu Mayonnaise, pg. 36, good mustard, ketchup, steam-fried onions and mushrooms, relish, lettuce, pickles, . . . mm-m-m-m.

Freeze for at least 48 hours:

2 lbs. reduced-fat, firm or medium-firm regular tofu

Thaw. Slice each pound block into 3 thick slices. Place the slices on a cookie sheet covered with a couple of folded, clean tea towels. Cover with more tea towels and another cookie sheet. Weigh down with something heavy for about 15-30 minutes. Now the tofu slices are ready for marinating.

For the marinade, mix together:

1½ cups of water
2 Tbsp. soy sauce or mushroom soy sauce
2 Tbsp. ketchup
2 tsp. Marmite, other yeast extract,
    or 1 Tbsp. dark miso
2 tsp. Kitchen Bouquet (opt.)
¼ tsp. garlic granules
¼ tsp. oregano
¼ tsp. basil
1 Tbsp. onion, chopped,
    ½ Tbsp. dried onion flakes,
    or ¼ tsp. onion powder

Pour over the tofu slices in a shallow baking pan in one layer. Cover and let marinate for several hours.

Just before serving, pan-fry on a lightly-greased heavy skillet until browned on both sides. Serve on buns with all the trimmings.

Per burger: Calories: 142, Protein 16 gm., Carbohydrates: 10 gm., Fat: 4 gm.

Creamy Pasta Sauce

Makes about 4½ cups (enough for about 2 lbs. pasta)

This sauce is thick, creamy, rich, and cheesy-tasting—one of my husband's favorites.

Combine in a blender:

> 1½ cups cold water
> 1 (10.5) oz. pkg. reduced-fat, extra-firm silken tofu,
>   or ½ lb. reduced-fat, medium-firm or firm regular tofu
> ¼ cup dry white wine,
>   or 3 Tbsp. water + 1 Tbsp. balsamic vinegar or lemon juice
> ⅓ cup nutritional yeast flakes
> 2 Tbsp. cornstarch
> 1½ Tbsp. chicken-style broth powder
> 2 tsp. salt
> 2 tsp. garlic granules
> 2½ Tbsp. sesame meal (opt.)

When smooth, add and blend again:

> 1½ cups hot or boiling water

Pour into a heavy saucepan, and stir over high heat constantly until it comes to a boil. Turn down and simmer on low for a few minutes.

Per ½ cup: Calories: 40, Protein: 2 gm., Carbohydrates: 4 gm., Fat: 0 gm.

Bright Idea . . .

Pasta Entreés

Use *Creamy Pasta Sauce* to make carbonnera by tossing with spaghetti, lots of freshly ground black pepper, 2 Tbsp. vegetarian bacon bits, and soy Parmesan. Also, serve with steam-fried vegetables, such as mushrooms and onions, chopped, frozen spinach (well-squeezed), other greens, and chopped, steamed dried tomatoes.

Bright Ideas . . .

If you have tortillas, salsa, and vegetables in your refrigerator and some canned beans on your shelf, dinner can be on the table in minutes.

Soft Vegetable Tacos and Burritos

See pg. 80 for methods for warming up tortillas. You can use commercially made corn tortillas or homemade *Flour Tortillas*, pg. 80. Have them warming and assemble your fillings from the following list:

steam-fried chopped onions, bell peppers, hot peppers, garlic, tomatoes

shredded lettuce or raw cabbage

chopped raw onions

steamed or frozen greens, heated

drained, cooked or canned pinto or black beans, or fat-free refried beans, heated

canned hominy, heated

Tofu Sour Cream, pg. 37

Low-Fat Guacamole, pg. 60

chopped fresh cilantro

Golden Sauce or *Tangy Cream Sauce*, pg. 41, heated

slivered seitan or *Oven-Fried Breast of Tofu*, pg. 22, heated

tomato salsa

Bean Dip, pg. 54, heated

leftover *Scrambled Tofu*, pg. 72, heated

crumbled, leftover *Savory Tofu Dinner Loaf*, pg. 105, heated

Enchilada Casserole Filling, pg. 116, heated

leftover chile, heated

leftover *Tofu Burger*, pg. 124, heated

New Orleans-style Red Beans, mixed with rice, pg. 132

Each person takes a warm tortilla, fills it with whatever fillings strike their fancy, folds it, and eats it out of hand.

Burritos are similar to soft tacos, but they are rolled up into a neat package. Use homemade *Flour Tortillas*, pg. 80. Place a 2"-wide strip of filling down the middle of the tortilla, fold over one side, pack in the filling, fold up the bottom, and roll over the rest of the tortilla.

Pineapple Sweet & Sour Stir-Fry

Serves 6

Sweet and sour stir-fry is a dish of Cantonese origin, but it's now an entrenched part of the American menu. Here's a delicious version, without the added oil.

In a large, lightly oiled wok, steam-fry over high heat:
> **1 large onion, cut into eighths with layers separated**
> **1 clove garlic, minced**
> **1 tsp. fresh ginger, minced**

When the onion begins to get slightly translucent:
> **1 (19 oz.) can unsweetened pineapple chunks**
>   **and their juice**
> **1 green bell pepper, seeded and cut into squares**
> **1 red bell pepper, seeded and cut into squares**
> **¼ cup sweetener of your choice**
> **¼ cup cider vinegar**
> **¼ cup ketchup**
> **1 Tbsp. soy sauce**

If you wish, you can add as optional items:
> **fresh carrots or celery, sliced on the diagonal**
> **fresh mushrooms, sliced**

Let the mixture come to a boil over high heat, and stir in:
> **2-3 cups any prepared tofu, seitan, or textured**
>   **vegetable protein chunks**
> **2 Tbsp. cornstarch dissolved in 2 Tbsp. of cold water**

Cook over high heat until the sauce thickens and the tofu, seitan or textured vegetable protein is heated through. Serve immediately over rice.

Per serving: Calories: 193, Protein: 9 gm., Carbohydrates: 38 gm., Fat: 2 gm.

Chick-pea a la King

Serves 6

This quick and easy home-style dish can be made into the pot pie variation on the next page.

In a large, heavy, lightly oiled or non-stick skillet, steam-fry:

> **1 cup fresh mushrooms, sliced**
> **1 cup celery, sliced**
> **½ cup onion, minced**

Meanwhile, combine in a blender until very smooth:

> **2½ cups water**
> **1 (10.5 oz.) pkg. reduced-fat, extra-firm silken tofu,**
> **   or ½ lb. reduced-fat, firm or medium-firm regular**
> **   tofu**
> **1 medium onion, peeled and cut into chunks**
> **¼ cup flour**
> **3 Tbsp. nutritional yeast**
> **4 tsp. sesame seeds**
> **1½ tsp. salt**
> **½ tsp. dried sage**
> **½ tsp. dried thyme**
> **½ tsp. garlic granules**
> **½ tsp. dried marjoram**

Add this to the steam-fried onion and garlic, and add:

> **2 cups cooked or canned chick-peas, drained**
> **½ cup frozen peas**
> **¼ cup fresh parsley, chopped,**
> **   or 1 tsp. paprika**
> **2-3 Tbsp. soy sauce**
> **black pepper to taste**

Simmer the mixture for 10 minutes, and serve over pasta, rice, or toast.

Per serving: Calories: 179, Protein: 11 gm., Carbohydrates: 27 gm., Fat: 3 gm.

Chick-pea a la King Casserole

Add **1 cup each diced cooked carrots and potatoes.** Bake in a shallow 2-quart casserole dish, topped with the *Drop Scone or Biscuit* dough on pg. 74, at 400°F. until golden (about 20 minutes).

Border Beans

Makes 6-8 servings

Soak in a large amount of water for at least 8 hours:

3 cups dried pinto beans

Discard the water and place the soaked beans in a large pot with:

8 cups vegetable or soybean broth
5 cloves garlic, chopped
1-3 dried red chiles, crumbled
2 tsp. dried oregano
a few dashes of liquid smoke

Bring to a boil, simmer for about 3 minutes, then turn the heat to low, cover, and simmer for 2-3 hours, or until the beans are very tender. The beans should be a bit "soupy" (the broth is delicious). If you have used a salt-free or low-salt broth, adjust for salt now.

To pressure cook these beans, cook the soaked beans at 15 lbs. pressure for 30 minutes. For unsoaked beans, use 11 cups of water and 8 broth cubes in a 6-quart pressure cooker, and pressure cook at 15 lbs. pressure for 1 hour.

Per serving: Calories: 109, Protein: 5 gm., Carbohydrates: 21 gm., Fat: 0 gm.

This is my vegetarian version of a recipe from my late mother-in-law, Ruth Clark. I use it as a basic bean recipe for any Mexican dish, but I always make a huge pot because I could honestly eat them every day. They're delicious with crusty bread and a green salad.

Chile Sin Carne

Serves 6 generously

This meatless chile is rich, dark, and spicy—it won first prize in a chile cook-off against several entries with meat!

Soak in enough water to cover for at least 8 hours:

2 cups dried pinto beans

Drain and rinse. In a large, heavy pot, mix the beans with:

4 cups water

¾ cup dry textured vegetable protein granules soaked in ¾ cup boiling water,
or ½-1 lb. frozen, reduced-fat firm regular tofu, thawed, squeezed, and crumbled

1 cup onions, minced

1 (6 oz.) can tomato paste

¼ cup soy sauce

1-2 Tbsp. chile powder (half ancho chile, if desired)

½ Tbsp. dried oregano

½ Tbsp. ground cumin

½ Tbsp. unsweetened cocoa powder

2 cloves garlic, minced

1 bay leaf

½ dried red chile pepper, crumbled

1 tsp. salt

½ tsp. sweetener of your choice

Bring this mixture to a boil, and simmer for 3 minutes. Then lower the heat, cover, and simmer until the beans are tender and the flavors are mixed (at least 2 hours or up to 4 hours, depending on how intense you like the flavor). To pressure cook, cook at 15 lbs. pressure for 20-25 minutes.

Taste and adjust the seasoning. If the mixture is too thin, thicken it by adding:

2-3 Tbsp. cornmeal

Let this simmer for another 5-10 minutes. Serve with crusty bread, corn bread, tortillas, or rice. It freezes well and leftovers are great in tacos.

Per serving: Calories: 277, Protein: 17 gm., Carbohydrates: 48 gm., Fat: 0 gm.

Hoppin' John

Serves 4-6

Soak for at least 8 hours in enough water to cover:

½ lb. dry black-eyed peas

Drain and rinse. Place the soaked beans in a large saucepan with:

2 cups water
1½ cups onions, chopped
1 large clove garlic, minced
1 bay leaf
½ tsp. ground black pepper
½ tsp. crushed dried red pepper
½ tsp. liquid smoke

Bring to a boil, let simmer for 3 minutes, then turn the heat to low, cover, and simmer for 30-60 minutes, or until the beans are tender as you like them. If you wish to pressure cook, cook at 15 lbs. pressure for 5-8 minutes.

Add:

1 Tbsp. soy sauce

Remove the bay leaf, and adjust salt to taste. Mash the beans slightly, and serve over steamed rice.

This spicy black-eyed pea dish is traditionally served on New Year's Day in the South, but this version is excellent any day of the year. Most recipes instruct you to add the rice to the beans, but I prefer the beans cooked separately and served over the rice.

Per serving: Calories: 59, Protein: 3 gm., Carbohydrates: 11 gm., Fat: 0 gm.

New Orleans-Style Red Beans

Serves 8

I'm from San Francisco, not New Orleans, but this is one of my favorite dishes. Mixed with rice, the leftover beans make a delicious burrito filling.

Soak in enough water to cover for at least 8 hours:

1 lb. small dried red beans (not kidney beans)

Drain and rinse. Place the beans in a large, heavy pot with enough water to cover with:

2 cups onions, minced
6 green onions, chopped
1 green bell pepper, seeded and chopped
1 cup fresh parsley, chopped
1 stalk celery, chopped
4 cloves garlic, chopped
½ cup tomato paste
1 large bay leaf
2-3 Tbsp. soy sauce
1½ tsp. ground coriander
1 tsp. ground cumin
½ tsp. EACH ground turmeric, dried oregano, dried thyme, and liquid smoke
pinch of cayenne pepper

Bring to a boil, simmer for 3 minutes, reduce heat to low, cover, and simmer for about 2 hours, or until the beans are soft and the liquid is "creamy." If you are pressure cooking, cook at 15 lbs. pressure for 20-25 minutes.

Taste and adjust for salt, pepper, and liquid smoke. Serve over steamed rice with cooked greens and Louisiana-style liquid hot sauce on the side.

Per serving: Calories: 117, Protein: 6 gm., Carbohydrates: 22 gm., Fat: 0 gm.

Chapter 7

Side Dishes and Accompaniments

While most of these dishes are used traditionally to accompany a main dish, most of them can *be* the main dish for everyday meals, particularly the more hearty potato, pasta, and grain recipes. One of our favorite meals is simply baked potatoes and steamed vegetables with some mushroom gravy. Another is scalloped potatoes with a salad. However, it may take some time to get your family used to the concept of all-vegetable or vegetable and grain meals. Be patient—after all, even spaghetti with tomato sauce is simply vegetables with a form of grain.

I most often steam, braise in vegetable broth, or stir-fry the vegetables I cook. Most vegetables are delicious seasoned with a little salt, pepper, and garlic. You can use a sprinkling of *Sesame Meal*, pg. 47, for a richer flavor. Toss them with *Corn Butter*, pg. 46; the garlic version is delicious on greens. Broccoli, cauliflower, and cabbage are wonderful with *Tangy Cream* or *Golden Sauce*, pg. 41. Be creative with other vegetarian seasonings and sauces: *Soy Cheesy Gomasio*, pg. 37, *Tofu Sour Cream*, pg. 37, *Tofu "Hollandaise,"* pg. 36, *Mock Hollandaise Sauce*, pg. 45, *Barbecue Sauce*, pg. 44, *Creamy Pasta Sauce*, pg. 125. You can also try commercial toppings like herbal salts, vegetarian bacon bits, Chinese sauces, and flavored vinegars. Leftover vegetables can be used in soups or mixed with a creamy sauce, topped with bread crumbs, and baked.

While most of us are familiar with corn, oats, rice, wheat, barley, and rye, there are many more exotic grains on the market today which deserve our consideration. Consult the cooking chart on pg. 187, and experiment with cooking grains with broth, herbs and spices, wine, tomatoes, and other seasonings for out-of-the ordinary, low-fat meals.

Bread Stuffing

Serves about 8 as a side dish

There are as many bread stuffings as there are cooks. I offer my own here not only because it's my favorite, but as a guide to adapting your own recipe to a fat-free version. I save my bread ends and scraps in the freezer until I have enough for a batch of stuffing. Then I serve it either baked in a large squash or in a baking pan and topped with Yeast Gravy, pg. 42, *and steam-fried mushrooms. This makes a great side dish with* Tofu Pot Pie, pg. 112, *mashed potatoes, and cranberry sauce for a memorable Thanksgiving or Christmas meal.*

In a large, heavy, lightly oiled skillet, steam-fry until softened:

> **1 cup onion, minced**
> **2 stalks celery with tops, chopped**
> **¼ cup fresh parsley, chopped (opt.)**

Turn off the heat and add:

> **¾ loaf of fat-free bread, cubed or crumbled**
> **2 tsp. dried sage leaves, freshly crumbled**
> **thyme, savory, or other favorite herb, to taste**
> **black pepper to taste**

Mix this well, then add:

> **1-1½ cups vegetable or soy broth**

These proportions may make a stuffing that seems a little moister than you're used to, but remember it won't be absorbing any fat or juices from a bird. Taste and adjust the seasonings.

You can bake the stuffing by packing it into a large, lightly oiled loaf, bundt pan, or muffin tins. Lightly brush the top with oil (Chinese sesame oil gives a nice "meaty" flavor), and cover with foil. Bake the loaf or bundt pan at 350°F for 30-60 minutes (depending on how crusty you like it) and muffin tins for 20-30 minutes. Remove the foil halfway through the baking time for a dryer stuffing; leave it on for a moister stuffing. Unmold the stuffing onto a platter, or serve right from the cooking dishes.

Per serving: Calories: 176, Protein: 6 gm., Carbohydrates: 37 gm., Fat: 0 gm.

Scalloped Potatoes

Serves 6-8

Although this is traditionally served as a side dish, you can use hearty optional ingredients to make this a delicious main dish as well.

Preheat the oven to 375°F. Peel and thinly slice:

8 large russet potatoes

Layer these in a lightly oiled 9" x 13" baking pan, sprinkling as you layer with:

salt and black pepper

flour (about 1 Tbsp. per layer—omit on top)

Combine in a blender until smooth:

3 cups soymilk

1 medium onion, cut in chunks

¼ cup nutritional yeast flakes

½ tsp. salt

Pour this over the potatoes, cover, and bake for 1 hour. Uncover and bake half an hour more.

Tasty optional ingredients to add while layering the potatoes are vegetarian bacon bits, *Fat-Free Sausage*, pg. 27, sliced onions, chopped chives, parsley, or other fresh herbs, dried herbs, steam-fried mushrooms, paprika and a bit of dry mustard, sliced green or red bell peppers, or steamed vegetables.

Per serving: Calories: 204, Protein: 6 gm., Carbohydrates: 43 gm., Fat: 1 gm.

Bright Idea . . .

Mashed Potatoes

Mashed potatoes are basic fare, but some of you may be at a loss as to how to season them without milk or butter. For 6 medium potatoes, whip in about ½ cup soymilk, *Tofu Sour Cream*, pg. 37, or *Tofu Milk*, pg. 39 . Season to taste with salt and black pepper. For extra flavor, boil a whole peeled head of garlic with the potatoes, and mash them together. Add minced fresh parsley or other herbs, steam-fried minced onions, vegetarian bacon bits, mashed cooked carrots, sweet potatoes, turnips, parsnips, or roasted rutabagas. Serve with gravy or *Corn Butter*, pg. 46.

Waffle Iron Hash Browns

Makes four 4-inch waffles

This is an easy and delicious hash brown variation that is a family favorite.

Preheat a lightly-oiled, non-stick waffle iron. In a medium bowl, mix together well:

> **4 cups raw potatoes (about 3-4 large potatoes), peeled and shredded**
> **2-4 Tbsp. fresh parsley, minced (opt.)**
> **2 Tbsp. Corn Butter, pg. 46 (opt.)**
> **1 Tbsp. egg replacer mixed with ¼ cup water**
> **1 Tbsp. nutritional yeast flakes**
> **1 Tbsp. flour**
> **1 Tbsp. onion granules**
> **1 tsp. salt**
> **½ tsp. garlic granules**

Pack half of this into the hot waffle iron, close the lid, and cook 12-15 minutes, or until golden and crispy. Repeat with the last half of the mixture.

NOTE: If you're in a hurry, or want a more simply seasoned "waffle," you may use just plain shredded potatoes. Cook for about 10 minutes.

These "waffles" can be frozen and crisped up again in a toaster-oven.

Per waffle: Calories: 134, Protein: 3 gm., Carbohydrates: 30 gm., Fat: 0 gm.

Potato Poppers

Makes 30 balls

These crispy little morsels are positively addictive! Serve them with gravy, ketchup, or chile sauce.

Preheat the oven to 350°F. Steam-fry in a small saucepan:

2 Tbsp. onion, chopped

Combine in a medium bowl:

1 cup cooked brown rice
1 cup leftover mashed potatoes
1 cup whole wheat bread crumbs
the steam-fried onion
2 Tbsp. tomato sauce or ketchup
½ tsp. salt

Mix well and roll the mixture into 30 balls about 1½ inches in diameter. Place them on lightly oiled, dark colored cookie sheets, far enough apart that they do not touch. Bake for 15 minutes; turn over and bake 10-15 minutes longer, until crisp and golden. Serve hot.

Per ball: Calories: 21, Protein: 0 gm., Carbohydrates: 4 gm., Fat: 0 gm.

Bright Idea . . .

Oven Hash Browns

Preheat the oven to 500°F. Spread grated raw potato, mixed with a bit of grated raw onion if desired, in a thin layer on a lightly oiled, dark cookie sheet, or shape large patties of the potato instead of covering the whole sheet. Flatten the potatoes firmly, and bake until they become golden-brown and crispy on one side. Turn the potatoes over and bake until the other side becomes golden brown and crispy.

Crispy Oven-Fried Potatoes

Serves 4

Preheat the oven to 400°F. Cut into French-fries, wedges, rounds, or chunks:

6 medium potatoes

Coat the potatoes with:

1 cup Roasting or Grilling Marinade, pg. 140

Spread the potatoes in a single layer on 2 lightly oiled, dark-colored cookie sheets. Bake for about 1 hour, turning them several times with a spatula until they are golden brown and crispy. Sprinkle with salt, herbal salt or seasoning, or seasoned salt, if you wish.

Per potato: Calories: 183, Protein: 2 gm., Carbohydrates: 43 gm., Fat: 0 gm.

Oven-Fried Onion Potatoes

VARIATIONS

Replace the marinade with **1 (1 oz.) packet vegetarian onion soup mix** rehydrated with **¾ cup boiling water**.

Spicy Mexican Potatoes

Sprinkle the potatoes with **paprika, salt, chile powder,** and **ground cumin** to taste before baking.

Cajun Potatoes

Sprinkle the potatoes with a **commercial Cajun spice mixture** or make your own by grinding in a blender **2 Tbsp. dried oregano, 2 Tbsp. garlic granules, 2 Tbsp. cayenne powder, 1 Tbsp. paprika, 1 Tbsp. dried ground cumin, 1 Tbsp. dried thyme, 1 Tbsp. onion granules,** and **1 tsp. ground black pepper**.

Roasting or Grilling Marinade

Makes about 3 cups

This very versatile marinade is similar to my fat-free salad dressing made with a cornstarch and water base. I keep a jar of it in my refrigerator at all times. It coats vegetables or potato wedges and both flavors and browns them in the oven. The result is very much like vegetables that are roasted or grilled with oil. Oven-baked "chips" are crunchy and golden; roasted vegetables are juicy and glazed. The marinade also works well as a coating for making crispy croutons. To make croutons, mix 2½ cups bread cubes with ¼ cup of the marinade and bake on oiled cookie sheets at 350°F until crispy.

In a heavy saucepan, mix:

2 cups cold water
2 Tbsp. cornstarch
2 Tbsp. "chicken-style" vegetable broth,
　or 2 vegetable broth cubes

Cook, stirring constantly, over high heat until the mixture has thickened and come to a boil. Add:

¾ cup lemon juice
grated zest of 1 lemon
2 Tbsp. herbal salt
4 large cloves garlic, crushed
1 tsp. dried oregano or other herb of choice,
　or 1 Tbsp. fresh herbs

For certain things you might want the stronger flavor of wine vinegar, cider or balsamic vinegar, or gourmet fruit vinegar instead of the lemon juice, but lemon juice is the most versatile. You can use fruit juice for some of the liquid, if you wish, or orange zest instead of the lemon zest. For a sweet glaze on root vegetables, add 2 tablespoons of maple syrup, honey, or other sweetener to ½ cup of the marinade.

Cut the vegetables into even-sized pieces. To grill, steam firm vegetables until half cooked. Marinate the vegetables for 4-6 hours before broiling or grilling. To roast, coat the vegetables well with the marinade. Toast in a shallow baking pan at 400°F for 45-60 minutes, turning the vegetables occasionally.

Per ½ cup: Calories: 18, Protein: 0 gm., Carbohydrates: 18 gm., Fat: 0 gm.

Grain and Noodle Pilaf

Serves 8

This homemade "rice-a-roni" is actually a common Middle Eastern dish, and it goes well with almost everything.

Heat a large, heavy, lightly oiled saucepan over high heat. Add:

> **2 cups long grain brown rice, converted rice, or bulgur wheat**
>
> **1 cup thin, whole wheat pasta, broken into small pieces**

Stir until the rice turns opaque. Add:

> **5 cups vegetable or soy broth**
>
> **1 tsp. ground cumin (opt.)**
>
> **½ tsp. dried oregano (opt.)**

Bring the mixture to a boil, cover, and reduce heat. Simmer for 45 minutes if you are using brown rice or 20 minutes if you are using converted rice or bulgur. Remove from the heat and let stand for 10 minutes before fluffing with a fork.

Per serving: Calories: 202, Protein: 5 gm., Carbohydrates: 43 gm., Fat: 0 gm.

Spanish Rice

Serves 6

In a large, lightly oiled skillet, steam-fry:

1 cup onions, chopped
2 cloves garlic, minced

When the onion softens, add:

1 cup basmati or converted rice
1 green bell pepper, seeded and chopped
¼ cup vegetarian bacon bits
1 Tbsp. salt
½ tsp. paprika
1 cup textured vegetable protein granules,
    rehydrated
        1 cup crumbled frozen tofu, seasoned with
            1 Tbsp. soy sauce,
        or 1 cup ground seitan

Stir-fry this for 2-3 minutes, then add:

2 cups tomato juice
dash cayenne pepper

Cover, bring to a boil, reduce heat, and simmer for 30 minutes.

Per serving: Calories: 165, Protein: 8 gm., Carbohydrates: 30 gm., Fat: 1 gm.

Corn "Oysters"

Makes sixteen 2-inch cakes

Process in a food processor until very finely minced:

> **2 cups corn kernels (about 3 large ears fresh corn or good quality canned or thawed frozen corn)**

Beat until stiff and foamy:

> **2 Tbsp. water**
> **2 tsp. egg replacer**

Pour the processed corn into a mixing bowl, and add:

> **the beaten egg replacer**
> **2 Tbsp. flour**
> **1 Tbsp. reduced-fat soymilk or other liquid**
> **¼ tsp. salt**
> **black pepper to taste**

Heat a non-stick or lightly oiled cast iron skillet or electric griddle over medium-high heat. Fry the mixture by spooning it onto the griddle and smoothing it out a little to make 2" wide cakes about ⅜" thick. Fry until crisp and golden brown on the bottom, then carefully loosen them and turn them over to brown the other side. If they are browning too fast, turn the heat down a little.

These can be reheated briefly in a 350°F oven.

Per cake: Calories: 22, Protein: 1 gm., Carbohydrates: 5 gm., Fat: 0 gm.

This is my version of a very old-fashioned corn fritter recipe. It's definitely best when you can use freshly picked corn, but also excellent with good quality canned or frozen corn kernels. You can eat these in the traditional manner with maple syrup, but I love them with salsa and Tofu Sour Cream, pg. 37, and sometimes with black beans for a complete and very colorful meal.

Chapter 8

Desserts

Nothing makes us crave desserts more than being told we can't eat them. You CAN eat them, but if you are trying to lose weight, don't eat even these low-fat desserts every day. Once or twice a week is probably the best average for most people. If you simply *must* have a dessert after dinner every day (and fresh fruit doesn't fill the bill), have *Caramel Cream Pudding*, pg. 164, *Chocolate Cornstarch Pudding*, pg. 163, or the *Berry and Banana Sherbet*, *Pineapple Sherbet*, or *Orange "Julia,"* pgs. 172-5. There are also a number of frozen dessert products on the market, but be sure a ½ cup serving contains under two grams of fat.

The desserts in this chapter are sweet enough to satisfy the average sweet tooth, but I have cut down the sugar in many of the traditional recipes. I have mixed feelings about sugar—while I don't believe that any research proves that sugar is to blame for most of our modern ills, it stands to reason that such concentrated, refined carbohydrate, stripped of its natural nutrients, may not be particularly good for us.

An excerpt from an excellent article about sweeteners which appeared in *Vegetarian Times* explains it well, "When consumed in moderation, sugar doesn't appear to be a problem for someone in good health. However, there *are* medical conditions in which sugar should be strictly limited, including diabetes, candida overgrowth, and heart disease. And though studies indicate that sugar doesn't cause hyperactivity, hypoglycemia, headaches, or myriad other problems popularly attributed to sweeteners, science doesn't always account for individual variation. You may very well notice a sugar sensitivity in yourself or other family members, in which case you'd be wise to cut back or eliminate sugar altogether."*

Many people have substituted a variety of "natural" sweeteners for sugar. For me, the major stumbling block to using these is price. This is further complicated by the fact that none of these sweeteners is as sweet as sugar, and most are more acidic as well. In order to achieve something near the sweetness of sugar, one must use half again, or even twice as much, of many of these sweeteners. This results in having to make adjustments with the liquids in the recipes, which doesn't always work.

The solution may be to try getting used to not-so-sweet sweets, but I don't really see the point if you are only eating desserts twice a week. I've cut out the fat and tried to cut down somewhat on the sugar, but I still like my sweets sweet.

One product that I do recommend is actually a type of sugar, but it is unrefined. Sucanat® (also know as Nutracane®) is dehydrated, organic sugar cane juice; nothing but the fiber and water is removed. It tastes just like a light brown sugar, but is somewhat nutritionally superior and is probably one of the only organic sweeteners (besides honey) on the market— Sucanat® can be used cup-for-cup instead of sugar.

If you do use sugar, and you are an "ethical vegetarian," you might take note of the fact that white *cane* sugar is bleached with bone ash made from beef bones. Beet sugar is not processed with bone ash. Brown and demerrara sugars (a very dark, coarse brown sugar) are merely bleached white sugars with molasses added (it is removed before the bleaching process.) So, if beet sugar is not available to you , the only truly vegetarian cane sugar is turbinado, which is not bleached. It is a very light beige color, and I use it instead of white sugar. For brown sugar, I use Sucanat® or turbinado sugar with a bit of blackstrap molasses added.

---

*Vegetarian Times, "Do You Really Want To Eat This? A Sugar Lover's Quest for the Truth About Her Sugar Habit," May 1993, pps. 74-79.

Turbinado sugar can be powdered by blending 1 cup with 1 tablespoon of cornstarch in the blender until very fine. It looks white when it's dry, but turns beige when liquid is added.

Blackstrap molasses is very rich in minerals, particularly calcium and iron. I love the taste of it, so I use it whenever molasses is called for. If you don't like the strong flavor, use unsulphured Barbados molasses.

Some vegetarians do not use honey because some large beekeepers kill their bees in the winter. It is possible to find local beekeepers who over-winter their bees, however, and who leave enough honey for the bees. Since honey is sweeter than sugar, you can use less, which makes the price more reasonable. Honey helps baked goods keep longer, but you have to be careful not to overbake them or the product may get too brown. It's a good idea to lower the temperature by 25°F when baking with honey in place of sugar.

Maple syrup is far too expensive to use regularly as a sweetener, except where the special taste of maple is desired.

In some recipes, a viable alternative to sugar or honey is frozen apple juice concentrate (and to a lesser extent, pine-apple, orange, and other frozen juice concentrates). The recipe must have a fair amount of liquid in it to start with. For each ½ cup of sugar and 1½ cups of liquid, substitute 1½ cups (a 12 oz. can) frozen apple juice concentrate, and add 1 teaspoon baking soda to counteract the acid in the juice. To use less liquid, boil it down by half. This sweet-ener works well in many muffin recipes, and it is reasonably priced.

Light and Easy Basic White Cake

Makes 12 cupcakes or one 8" tube cake

Preheat the oven to 325°F. Lightly grease 12 muffins cups or an 8" tube or bundt pan. In a blender, mix until very smooth:

**1 (10.5 oz.) pkg. reduced-fat firm silken tofu,
  or 8 oz. reduced-fat, firm regular tofu
1 cup sugar of choice or Sucanat®
½ cup water
1 Tbsp. vanilla or other extract
1 Tbsp. lemon juice**

In a medium bowl, mix together:

**1¼ cups unbleached flour or whole wheat pastry flour
6 Tbsp. oat flour (*do not* substitute more wheat
  flour—see pg. 19)
1 tsp. baking soda
1 tsp. baking powder
¾ tsp. salt**

Pour the contents of the blender into the bowl, and mix briefly but thoroughly. Scrape into the prepared pan or muffin tins. (Paper muffin cups stick to very low-fat mixtures, so it's better not to use them.) Bake 20-25 minutes for cupcakes and about 45 minutes for a bundt cake—until an inserted toothpick comes out clean. Do not overbake. Cool on a rack.

Per cupcake: Calories: 132, Protein: 3 gm., Carbohydrates: 27 gm., Fat: 1 gm.

Spice Cake

Use brown sugar or Sucanat®. Add to the dry ingredients **1½ tsp. cinnamon, ½ tsp. powdered ginger, ½ tsp. ground cloves,** and **¼ tsp. nutmeg.** You can also add **¾ cup currants or chopped raisins** if you like.

This cake is light and moist and can be used as a basis for many other cakes: coffee cakes, streusel cakes, upside-down cakes, etc. Add grated citrus zest or extracts of your choice, spices, or substitute juices for water. Use it with a fruit sauce as "cottage pudding"—the choices are endless. I call this "white" cake because the color depends upon the type of sweetener and flour you use. I generally use turbinado sugar, which results in a "beige" cake. Whatever color, it can stand in for sponge or pound cakes in trifle and similar recipes.

One caution: *this does not work well when cooked in a flat cake pan. It needs to be made into cupcakes or in a tube or bundt pan with a hole in the middle.*

Light and Easy Chocolate Cake

Makes 12 cupcakes or one 8" tube cake

This is made in the same way as Basic White Cake *and, if anything, is even more tender. If you prefer to use carob instead of cocoa powder, use coffee or a coffee substitute instead of the water for a less cloying taste.* Sucanat® *works well in this recipe.*

One caution: this does not work well when cooked in a flat cake pan. It needs to be made into cup-cakes or in a tube or bundt pan with a hole in the middle.

Preheat the oven to 325°F. Lightly grease 12 muffins cups or an 8" tube or bundt pan.

In a blender, mix until very smooth:

> 1 (10 oz.) pkg. reduced-fat firm silken tofu,
>   or 8 oz. reduced-fat, firm regular tofu
> 1 cup sugar or Sucanat®
> ½ cup water, coffee, or coffee substitute
> 6 Tbsp. unsweetened cocoa powder
> 1 Tbsp. vinegar
> 1 Tbsp. vanilla

In a medium bowl, mix together:

> 1¼ cups unbleached flour or whole wheat pastry
>   flour
> 1 tsp. baking soda
> 1 tsp. baking powder
> ½ tsp. salt

Pour the contents of the blender into the bowl, and mix together briefly but thoroughly. Scrape into the prepared pan or muffin tins. (Paper muffin cups stick to very low-fat mixtures, so it's better not to use them.) Bake 20-25 minutes for cupcakes and about 45 minutes for the tube or bundt cake—until an inserted toothpick comes out clean. Do not overbake. Cool on a rack.

Per cupcake: Calories: 128, Protein: 3 gm., Carbohydrates: 27 gm., Fat: 1 gm.

Lean Cocoa Frosting

Makes about 2½ cups

This is the perfect chocolate icing—smooth, glossy, rich-tasting, and virtually fat-free!.

Mix together in a blender:

> **1 cup reduced-fat soymilk or other non-dairy milk, or ½ cup soymilk + ½ cup coffee or coffee substitute**
>
> **¾ cup granulated sweetener of choice or Sucanat®**
>
> **⅔ cup unsweetened cocoa**
>
> **⅓ cup cornstarch**

Pour into a heavy, medium saucepan, and stir constantly over medium heat with a wooden spoon, scraping the bottom and sides often, for about 7 minutes until thick and glossy.

Remove the pan from the heat, and add:

> **1 tsp. vanilla extract**

Beat the mixture with a wire whisk to remove any lumps. Cool the mixture completely, stirring occasionally. You can refrigerate it if it's made ahead of time, but bring it to room temperature before frosting the cake. Beat until smooth again.

If the mixture is too thick or not sweet enough, whip in a little maple syrup or other liquid sweetener.

Per 2 Tbsp.: Calories: 51, Protein: 1 gm., Carbohydrates: 11 gm., Fat: 0 gm.

White Glaze

Makes ½ cup

This is delicious on Cinnamon Buns, pg. 82, and other sweet breads, cakes, cupcakes, or tea breads.

In a small bowl, mix together thoroughly:

**½ cup powdered soymilk (plain or vanilla)
or other powdered non-dairy milk powder
(preferably a low-fat version)
2-4 Tbsp. honey or other liquid sweetener
¼ tsp. vanilla extract or other flavoring extract**

For a thin glaze, spread this on hot bread or cake. For a thicker glaze or icing, spread it after the bread or cake has cooled.

Per Tbsp.: Calories: 57, Protein: 4 gm., Carbohydrates: 10 gm., Fat: 0 gm.

Bright Idea . . .

Orange or Lemon Glaze

In a small saucepan, boil 3 tablespoons orange or lemon juice (preferably fresh) and either ¼ cup honey or ½ cup sugar for 3 minutes. Brush or spoon over hot cake, cupcakes, muffins, or tea breads.

Cream Cheeze Icing

Makes about 1½ cups

In a small saucepan, soak for 5 minutes:

> **1 Tbsp. cold water**
> **1 Tbsp. lemon juice**
> **½ tsp. agar powder,**
> > **or 1 Tbsp. agar flakes**

Stir in:

> **¼ cup honey or other liquid sweetener**

Add to the pan:

> **1 (10.5 oz.) pkg. reduced-fat, extra-firm silken tofu,**
> > **crumbled**

Stir over high heat until the tofu is hot (this is important so that the agar doesn't gel too fast). Pour the mixture into the blender with:

> **1 tsp. vanilla extract,**
> > **or ½ tsp. coconut or almond extract**

Blend until very smooth. Chill in a bowl until the mixture is spreadable, but not completely cold. Frost the cake or cupcakes, and chill again.

Per 2 Tbsp.: Calories: 33, Protein: 1 gm., Carbohydrates: 5 gm., Fat: 0 gm.

VARIATION

Cream Cheese-Fruit Icing

Fold into the *Cream Cheese Icing* mixture after it is blended, but while it is still hot **1 small banana mashed with 1 tsp. lemon juice, or 1 cup well-drained crushed pineapple.**

Yeasted Pastry

Makes enough for one 9" double crust pie (serves 8)

It's impossible to make a flaky pastry without fat. I use the Crumb Crust, pg. 159, for tofu "cheesecakes" and cream pies, and some fruit pies, but I really like this tender yeasted pastry for cooked fruit pies and quiches. You can make a conventional double crust pie, but I prefer to make a "free-form" pie, which is rolled into one large circle with the edges folded up over the filling and baked free-standing on a cookie sheet rather than a pie pan. This makes a lovely, home-style dessert.

In a medium bowl or a food processor, let stand for 5 minutes:

> ½ cup warm soymilk,
>> or 1 Tbsp. soymilk powder mixed with ½ cup warm water
>
> 3 Tbsp. warm, leftover mashed potatoes,
>> or 3 Tbsp. instant mashed potato flakes mixed with 2½ Tbsp. boiling water
>
> ½ Tbsp. honey or other liquid sweetener
>
> 1 tsp. baking yeast

Add:

> 1¼ cups unbleached flour (not pastry flour),
>> or 1 cup unbleached flour plus ¼ cup whole wheat flour
>
> ¼ tsp. salt

Knead for 5 minutes or process in the food processor for 30 seconds.

Place the dough in a greased bowl, cover with plastic, and let rise in a warm place until doubled (30-60 minutes) or in the refrigerator for up to 24 hours. If refrigerating, oil the top of the dough lightly, and cover well with plastic to prevent drying out.

To make a double crust pie, preheat the oven to 350°F, divide the dough in half, and roll one half to fit the bottom of a lightly greased 9" pie plate. Fill the pie with your favorite filling, and cover with the second half of the dough, rolled to fit the top. Crimp the edges together, and cut slits in the top for steam to escape. Bake immediately for 25-30 minutes or until golden. The pie may be glazed before baking with soymilk and a sprinkling of sugar, or after baking with maple syrup or apple juice concentrate.

To make a "free-form" pie, preheat the oven to 350°F, roll the dough out on a floured surface into a 16" circle, and place it carefully on a lightly greased cookie sheet or pizza pan. Make sure there are no holes or excessively thin spots in the dough. Pile the filling in the center, and drape the edges up over the filling, "pleating" it attractively and leaving about a 5" hole in the center. Bake immediately for about 25-30 minutes or until golden, glazing it either before or after baking as for 9" pie above.

You can make a deep-dish pie by placing the filling in an empty, deep-dish pie pan and using a top crust only.

You can make twice the amount of dough by doubling all the ingredients except the yeast.

Per serving: Calories: 78, Protein: 2 gm., Carbohydrates: 17 gm., Fat: 0 gm.

Pie Fillings

Makes enough for one 9" pie (serves 8)

Apple Pie Filling

Mix together in a bowl:

> **8 large, tart apples, peeled if desired, cored, and
> sliced**
> **½ cup granulated sweetened of your choice or
> Sucanat®, or ⅓ cup honey**
> **2 Tbsp. flour,
> or 1 Tbsp. cornstarch**
> **1 Tbsp. lemon juice**
> **½ tsp. cinnamon or to taste**
> **pinch nutmeg**
> **pinch salt**
> **¼-½ cup raisins (opt.)**

*Per serving: Calories: 130, Protein: 0 gm., Carbohydrates: 31 gm.,
Fat: 0 gm.*

Peach Pie Filling

Mix together in a bowl:

> **5 cups ripe, sweet peaches, sliced**
> **¾ cup granulated sweetener of your choice or
> Sucanat®**
> **2 Tbsp. flour,
> or 1 Tbsp. cornstarch**
> **1 tsp. lemon juice**
> **¼ tsp. EACH cinnamon, nutmeg, almond extract,
> and salt**

*Per serving: Calories: 109, Protein: 1 gm., Carbohydrates: 27 gm.,
Fat: 0 gm.*

Pumpkin Pie

Serves 8

I've been serving this pie for several years, and no one realizes that it's not only non-dairy and egg-free, but very low in fat. It's very important to make this the day before you serve it so that the filling can set properly.

Prepare:

> ½ recipe Yeasted Pastry, pg. 152

Roll it out to fit a lightly greased 9" pie pan, place it in the pan, and crimp the edges. Preheat the oven to 350°F.

Mix well in a blender:

> 2 cups solid-pack, canned pumpkin,
>   or cooked pumpkin, mashed and well-drained
> 1 cup reduced-fat soymilk or other non-dairy milk
> ¾ cup brown sugar or Sucanat®,
>   or ½ cup honey
> ¼ cup cornstarch
> 1 Tbsp. molasses or blackstrap molasses
> 1 tsp. cinnamon
> 1 tsp. vanilla extract
> ½ tsp. powdered ginger
> ½ tsp. nutmeg
> ½ tsp. salt
> ¼ tsp. ground allspice or cloves

When the mixture is smooth, pour it into the prepared crust. Bake for 60 minutes, covering the edges of the pie crust with foil if they begin to brown too quickly. Cool on a rack, then refrigerate overnight before serving. Top with *Whipped Soy Cream*, pg. 38.

Per serving: Calories: 145, Protein: 2 gm., Carbohydrates: 34 gm., Fat: 0 gm.

Fruit Kuchen

Serves 8-12

A kuchen (pro-nounced "koo-ken") is a large fruit tart of German origin, usually made with a cookie crust and a sour cream and egg custard. My version has a yeasted crust and a creamy tofu custard. It's hard to believe that anything so rich-tasting can be low in fat!

Prepare:

a double recipe of Yeasted Pastry, pg. 152

When the pastry has risen once, preheat the oven to 400°F, and roll the pastry out to fit an oiled 10" x 15" cookie sheet. Press it to fit the pan with a small rim around the edges like a pizza.

Arrange over the pastry in neat rows or an artistic pattern:

12 ripe peaches, pears, or nectarines, sliced,
  or about 24 large plums or apricots, pitted and sliced (peeled if desired),
  or any other fresh fruit of your choice,
  or an equivalent amount of frozen or canned fruit, alone or in combination (thaw and drain frozen fruit and use fruit canned in fruit juice)

Sprinkle the fruit with:

½ cup granulated sweetener of your choice or Sucanat®,
  or ⅓ cup honey
1 tsp. cinnamon

Bake this for 10-15 minutes. Meanwhile, mix in a blender until smooth:

1½ (10.5) oz. pkgs. reduced-fat, extra-firm silken tofu,
  or ¾ lb. reduced-fat, firm or medium-firm regular tofu, crumbled
6 Tbsp. water
6 Tbsp. granulated sweetener of your choice or Sucanat®
2 Tbsp. lemon juice
pinch salt

Remove the pan from the oven, and drizzle the tofu mixture evenly over the fruit. Smooth it out if necessary. Lower the heat to 375°F, and bake 20 more minutes or until the tofu is set.

Cool on a rack. Serve warm or cold, cut into squares (use a very sharp knife).

Per serving: Calories: 301, Protein: 8 gm., Carbohydrates: 61 gm., Fat: 1 gm.

Fruit Syrup

Makes 2-3 cups

Use on puddings, cakes, crepes, waffles, or pancakes.

Puree in a blender:

> **6 cups fresh berries or other fruit, washed, trimmed, and sliced**
> **1 (6 oz.) can frozen apple juice concentrate**

Pour this into a medium saucepan, and add:

> **1 tsp. cornstarch dissolved in 2 Tbsp. cold water, juice, or wine**

Stir over high heat until the sauce thickens and clears. Add:

> **1-3 tsp. vanilla, orange, or lemon extract,**
> **1 tsp. orange or lemon zest, grated,**
> **½ tsp. almond extract,**
> **   or 2 Tbsp. brandy, rum, or fruit liqueur**

Serve hot or cold.

Per ¼ cup: Calories: 63, Protein: 1 gm., Carbohydrates: 14 gm., Fat: 0 gm.

Tofu Cheezecake Pie

Serves 8

*Even people who
haven't been able to
warm up to tofu in
any other form will
find this delicious.
Make this the day
before serving.*

Prepare and bake for 5 minutes:

1 Crumb Crust, pg. 159

Preheat the oven to 350°F. In a blender, mix until very smooth:

1 lb. reduced-fat, medium-firm regular tofu
**⅓ cup granulated sweetener of your choice or
      Sucanat®**
2 Tbsp. reduced-fat soymilk or other non-dairy milk
**2 Tbsp. flour,
      or 1 Tbsp. cornstarch**
1 Tbsp. lemon juice
1½ Tbsp. Sesame Meal, pg. 47
**1 Tbsp. light miso,
      or ¼ tsp. salt**
1 tsp. vanilla extract
½ tsp. almond extract
½ tsp. lemon zest, grated

Pour the tofu mixture into the prepared crust, and bake for about 50 minutes or until the tofu mixture is set. Cool on a rack, then refrigerate until well-chilled.

To make a fruit topping, mix in a small saucepan:

2 cups frozen berries or other fruit
**¼ -½ cup granulated sweetener, honey, or other
      sweetener**
1 Tbsp. cornstarch mixed with 2 Tbsp. water

Stir over high heat until the mixture has boiled and thickened. Taste for sweetness. If you like, add a bit of appropriately flavored fruit juice liqueur to the topping.

Spoon the fruit topping over the cheezecake pie, and refrigerate until the topping is cool. Serve with *Whipped Soy Cream*, pg. 38, if you like.

Per serving: Calories: 269, Protein: 10 gm., Carbohydrates: 52 gm., Fat: 1 gm.

Crumb Crust
Makes one 9" pie crust (serves 8)

Preheat oven to 350°F.

Grind in a blender or food processor to make fine crumbs:

> **2 cups Grapenuts® cereal, or Light and Easy Cake crumbs (pgs. 147-48) which have been dried like breadcrumbs**

Pour the crumbs into a small bowl, and add:

> **¼ cup maple syrup or fruit concentrate syrup**
>
> **¼ tsp. coconut or almond extract (opt.)**

Mix well with a fork. Press the sweetened crumbs evenly onto the bottom and sides of a lightly greased, 9" pie pan, covering completely.

Pre-bake for 5 minutes before filling and baking your pie, or bake unfilled for 10 minutes before adding an unbaked filling.

Per serving: Calories: 131, Protein: 3 gm., Carbohydrates: 30 gm., Fat: 0 gm.

Frypan Cookies or Crispy Bars

This is from an old recipe dating back to the '30s.

Makes 18 one-inch bars

Mix together in a heavy, small skillet:

>   ¾ cup pitted dates, chopped
>   ½ cup granulated sweetener of your choice or Sucanat®
>   1 Tbsp. powdered egg replacer beaten with ¼ cup water

Cook, stirring, over medium heat for 8 minutes, or until thickened. Mix in:

>   1 cup natural, crispy rice cereal
>   1 cup natural flaked corn cereal, crushed (2 scant cups whole flakes)
>   1 tsp. vanilla extract

Either press into a greased, 8" square pan, cool, and cut into bars, or roll the warm mixture into balls or logs. If you like, roll the balls or logs in finely ground *No-Oil Granola*, pg. 73.

Per bar: Calories: 61, Protein: 1 gm., Carbohydrates: 14 gm., Fat: 0 gm.

VARIATIONS

Chocolate Frypan Cookies or Crispy Bars

Add **¼ cup unsweetened cocoa** to the date mixture. Continue as for regular *Frypan Cookies*.

Nice 'n Crispy Squares

Add cocoa as for *Chocolate Frypan Cookies*. Use **1½ cups natural, crispy rice cereal** and **½ cup crushed, natural flaked corn cereal (1 scant cup whole flakes)**. You can add **½ teaspoon peanut butter flavoring,** or **coconut** or **almond extract**.

Basic Bread Pudding

Serves 6

For all my fellow bread pudding lovers out there.

Preheat the oven to 350°F. Mix in a blender:

1¾ cups soymilk
⅓ cup granulated sweetener of your choice,
    or ¼ cup honey
1½ Tbsp. nutritional yeast flakes
¼ tsp. salt

Place in a greased, 8" square pan:

4 cups stale bread, cubed or thinly sliced,
    or stale cake or fruitcake

Do not use bread that has dried out to the point of being hard. If the crusts are very hard, trim them off.

Pour the blended mixture over the bread, and let stand for 20 minutes. Set the 8" pan inside of a larger pan with hot water in it. Sprinkle the top of the pudding with:

cinnamon and/or nutmeg

Bake for 30 minutes. Serve plain, with fruit, or a pudding sauce (see pgs. 169-70).

Per serving: Calories: 152, Protein: 5 gm., Carbohydrates: 27 gm., Fat: 2 gm.

English "Bread and Butter" Pudding

VARIATIONS

Use thinly sliced bread and sprinkle **2 Tbsp. currants** between the layers of bread. Sprinkle the top of the pudding with nutmeg only.

Creole Bread Pudding

Use cubes of French or Italian bread with the crusts removed. Add **1 teaspoon vanilla extract** to the blended mixture. Serve with *Brown Sugar Pudding Sauce*, made with brandy or rum (or brandy or rum extract), pg. 169.

Tofu Chocolate Mousse

This tastes much richer than it is. It's great topped with banana slices and Whipped Soy Cream, pg. 38.

Serves 4

Mix in a small saucepan, and stir over high heat until dissolved:

> **6 Tbsp. granulated sweetener of your choice or Sucanat®**
> **3 Tbsp. strong coffee, coffee substitute, or water**

Stir in:

> **4 Tbsp. unsweetened cocoa**

Stir until a paste forms. Place this in the blender with:

> **1 (10.5 oz.) pkg. reduced-fat, firm silken tofu**
> **1 tsp. vanilla extract**
> **pinch salt**
> **1 Tbsp. rum, coffee or chocolate liqueur, or other liqueur (opt.)**
> **¼ tsp. cinnamon (opt.)**

Blend the mixture until very smooth. Pour into 4 pudding dishes, cover, and chill for several hours.

Per serving: Calories: 121, Protein: 3 gm., Carbohydrates: 20 gm., Fat: 0 gm.

VARIATIONS

Frozen Chocolate Tofulato

Double the recipe for *Tofu Chocolate Mousse*, and add **½ cup reduced-fat soymilk or other non-dairy milk.** Follow the directions for your ice cream maker.

Fudgesicles

Prepare *Tofu Chocolate Mousse*, but omit the liqueur and coffee, and use only 2-3 tablespoons cocoa. Add **5 tablespoons water.** Freeze in popsicle molds.

Chocolate Tofu Pie

Double the recipe for *Tofu Chocolate Mousse*, and use **reduced-fat, extra-firm silken tofu**. Spread the mousse in a baked *Crumb Crust*, pg. 159. Chill thoroughly and serve topped with *Whipped Soy Cream*, pg. 38.

Chocolate Cornstarch Pudding

Serves 4

This is one of my childhood favorites and is very easy to make.

Mix in a blender:

> **2 cups reduced-fat soymilk or other non-dairy milk**
> **¼ cup granulated sweetener of your choice or Sucanat®**
> **3 Tbsp. unsweetened cocoa**
> **2 Tbsp. cornstarch**

When the mixture is well blended, pour it into a medium saucepan with a heavy bottom. Stir it constantly over high heat with a wooden spoon until it thickens and comes to a boil. Turn down the heat to low, cover, and cook for 1 minute.

Stir in:

> **1 tsp. vanilla extract**

Pour into 4 pudding dishes, cover, and refrigerate for several hours.

Per serving: Calories: 122, Protein: 3 gm., Carbohydrates: 24 gm., Fat: 2 gm.

Caramel Cream Pudding

Serves 6

This custard-like dessert makes an excellent ending to a heavy dinner. I like to top it with fruit as an edible decoration.

In a small saucepan with a heavy bottom, bring to a boil over low heat:

> **5 Tbsp. granulated sweetener of your choice or Sucanat®**
> **3 Tbsp. water**

Simmer uncovered for 5 minutes. Remove from heat. Working quickly, place in a blender:

> **⅔ cup reduced-fat, firm or medium-firm regular tofu, crumbled**
> **1 Tbsp. of the sugar syrup from above**
> **4 tsp. vanilla extract**
> **pinch of salt**

Set this aside and pour the rest of the syrup evenly into 6 custard molds. Rotate each one to coat the base and sides with the syrup. Set aside.

Into the same saucepan, place:

> **2½ cups reduced-fat soymilk or other non-dairy milk**
> **1½ Tbsp. agar flakes,**
>   **or ¾ tsp. agar powder**

Bring this quickly to a boil, stirring constantly, then reduce the heat and simmer for 5 minutes. Continue to stir. Add this hot soymilk to the mixture in the blender, and blend it to a smooth cream. Stir down the bubbles.

Pour the blended mixture into the coated molds, and skim off any foam. Cover the molds with plastic wrap, and refrigerate them until serving time.

To unmold, dip the bottom of each mold briefly into boiling water, then remove the plastic wrap, and turn upside down on a dessert plate. The pudding should slide out easily. Pour any syrup left in the bottom of the mold over the pudding, and decorate with fruit, edible flowers, mint, or lemon balm leaves, etc.

Per serving: Calories: 98, Protein: 4 gm., Carbohydrates: 17 gm., Fat: 1 gm.

VARIATION

Coconut Custard

This is very similar to a dessert served in South American countries and in Southeast Asia, so it makes an excellent ending to many exotic meals. I like to serve it with pineapple chunks. Omit 2 teaspoons of vanilla, and add **2 tablespoons granulated sweetener** and **¾ teaspoon coconut extract** to the blender mixture.

Hot Fudge Pudding Cake

Serves 6

If you're in the mood for something sweet, gooey, and chocolatey, this is easy to whip up in a hurry, and you can eat it straight out of the oven.

Preheat the oven to 350°F. In a small bowl, mix together:

1 cup whole wheat pastry flour
¼ cup granulated sweetener of your choice or Sucanat®
¼ cup oat flour
¼ cup unsweetened cocoa
2 tsp. baking powder
¼ tsp. salt

Stir in, but do not over-beat:

¾ cup reduced-fat soymilk or other non-dairy milk
2 tsp. vanilla extract,
    or ½ tsp. almond or coconut extract
2 Tbsp. coffee or chocolate liqueur (opt.)

With wet fingers, spread the batter into a lightly greased or non-stick 8" square pan. Sprinkle the top evenly with a mixture of:

1 cup granulated sweetener of your choice or Sucanat®
¼ cup unsweetened cocoa

Over the top, pour on but don't stir in:

2 cups boiling coffee or coffee substitute

Bake for 35 minutes. The cake will be on top, with a sauce underneath. Serve plain or with *Whipped Soy Cream*, pg. 38.

Per serving: Calories: 274, Protein: 5 gm., Carbohydrates: 60 gm., Fat: 2 gm.

Fruit Pudding Cake

Omit the cocoa from both the batter and the topping. Add **1 cup chopped fresh fruit or ½ cup dried fruit** to the batter. Use **fruit juice** instead of soymilk in the batter, if you like. You can add some **grated citrus rind** to the batter. Use only **1¾ cups boiling water** instead of the coffee.

Lemon Pudding Cake

Omit the cocoa from the batter and the topping. Use **white or turbinado sugar** for the sweetener. Omit the vanilla extract and add **1 tablespoon grated lemon zest**. For the liquid in the topping, omit the coffee and use **¼ cup lemon juice with 1½ cups boiling water**.

Date Pudding Cake

Omit the cocoa from the batter and the topping. Add **1 cup chopped dates** to the batter. Omit the vanilla extract, if you like. Instead of the coffee, use **1¾ cups boiling water** in the topping.

Old-Fashioned Rice Pudding

Serves 6

This traditional dish was always made without eggs; it's basically a milk dish thickened with rice.

Preheat the oven to 300°F. Pour into an oiled, 2-quart casserole:

> **4 cups reduced-fat soymilk**
> **¼ cup short grain brown rice**
> **¼ cup granulated sweetener of your choice or Sucanat®,**
> **   or 3 Tbsp. honey**
> **¼ tsp. salt**
> **⅓ cup raisins or currants (opt.)**

Sprinkle the top of the mixture with:

> **nutmeg or cinnamon**

Bake the pudding for 20 minutes, then stir. Bake uncovered for 2½ hours if made in a metal pan, 3 hours if baked in glass or ceramic. The pudding will seem a bit runny, but it will thicken up as it cools.

Serve plain or with *Whipped Soy Cream*, pg. 38, and/or fruit, fruit syrup, or maple syrup. You can add many optional ingredients to this basic recipe: vanilla or other extracts, rum or liqueurs, grated citrus zest, other dried fruits such as apricots, or ½ tsp. coconut extract.

Per serving: Calories: 128, Protein: 4 gm., Carbohydrates: 26 gm., Fat: 1 gm.

Lemon Pudding Sauce

Makes about 1¼ cups

In a small saucepan, stir over high heat until it thickens:

1 cup water
½ cup sugar,
 or ⅓ cup honey
1 Tbsp. cornstarch
pinch of salt

Boil for 1 minutes. Stir in:

juice of half a lemon
1 tsp. lemon zest, grated

Per ¼ cup: Calories: 79, Protein: 0 gm., Carbohydrates: 20 gm., Fat: 0 gm.

Brown Sugar Pudding Sauce

Makes about 1¼ cups

In a small saucepan, stir over high heat:

1 cup water
½ cup brown sugar or Sucanat®
1 Tbsp. cornstarch
pinch of salt

When it thickens, allow to boil for 1 minute. Stir in:

1 tsp. vanilla extract, or rum or brandy flavoring,
 or 3 Tbsp. rum, brandy, or flavored liqueur

Per ¼ cup: Calories: 60, Protein: 0 gm., Carbohydrates: 15 gm., Fat: 0 gm.

Orange Pudding Sauce

Makes about 1¾ cups

In a small saucepan, stir over high heat:

> **1 cup orange juice**
> **½ cup water**
> **⅓ cup sugar,**
>   **or ¼ cup honey**
> **1½ tsp. cornstarch**
> **1 tsp. lemon juice**
> **½ tsp. lemon jest, grated**
> **¼ tsp. salt**

Stir until it thickens, then allow to boil for one minute.

Per ¼ cup: Calories: 52, Protein: 0 gm., Carbohydrates: 12 gm., Fat: 0 gm.

Basic Tofu Ice Cream

Makes about 5 cups

These ice creams freeze up quite solidly, so let them, sit out of the freezer for ½ an hour before serving.

In a small saucepan, dissolve over high heat:

1 cup sugar

4 Tbsp. water

NOTE: If you wish, you can use ⅔ cup honey instead of the sugar and water syrup. Pour the syrup or honey in a blender with:

4 (10.5 oz.) pkgs. soft silken tofu,
   or 2 lbs. reduced-fat, medium-firm regular tofu
      + 1 cup water

2 Tbsp. vanilla extract

¼ tsp. salt

Blend until the mixture is very smooth, then chill thoroughly. Freeze according to the directions for your ice cream maker.

Per cup: Calories: 238, Protein: 5 gm., Carbohydrates: 37 gm., Fat: 1 gm.

Maple Tofu Ice Cream

VARIATIONS

Use **2½ cups maple syrup** in place of the sugar or honey; use the medium-firm tofu and omit the 1 cup water used with it.

Coffee Tofu Ice Cream

Use **1½ cups sugar or Sucanat®** dissolved in **⅔ cup strong coffee or coffee substitute.** Use the medium-firm tofu and omit ½ cup of the water used with it. You can add **¼ cup rum or coffee liqueur**, if you wish.

VARIATIONS

Chocolate Tofu Ice Cream

See the *Chocolate Tofulato* variation under the *Tofu Chocolate Mousse* recipe, pg. 162.

Fruit Sherbet

Add **4-5 cups pureed, sliced or chopped fresh, frozen, or canned fruit, ¼ cup lemon juice, and ⅛ teaspoon more salt.** Use the medium firm tofu, and omit the 1 cup water used with it.

Orange Sherbet

Add **1 cup orange juice concentrate** and **¼ cup lemon juice.** Use the medium-firm tofu and omit ½ cup of the water used with it.

Bright Idea . . .

Frozen Brownie Pie

This makes a great birthday cake. Make a batch of *Light and Easy Chocolate Cake* or *Cupcakes*, pg. 148. Cut the cake horizontally to make ½"-¾"-thick slices. Line a baking pan of whatever shape you wish with the slices, filling the gaps with cake scraps. Spread the cake with *Basic Tofu Ice Cream* (you can also use the maple, coffee, or fruit variations, or even the *Chocolate Tofulato*, if you really love chocolate), as thick as you like. Wrap with plastic wrap, and freeze solid. Top the pie with *Whipped Soy Cream*, pg. 38, and sprinkle with some of the chocolate cake crumbs. Freeze until serving time. Serve with *Chocolate Sauce*, pg. 177, plain or coffee-flavored.

Frozen Mocha Tofu Ice

Makes 5 cups

In a small saucepan, dissolve over high heat:

2 cups strong liquid coffee or coffee substitute
¾ cup granulated sweetener of your choice or
    Sucanat®

Stir in :

¼ cup unsweetened cocoa

Stir until smooth and let simmer for 1 minute.

Pour into a blender with:

1½ (10.5 oz.) pkgs. reduced-fat, firm silken tofu
1 Tbsp. vanilla extract
⅛ tsp. salt

Blend until very smooth, then chill thoroughly. Freeze according to the directions with your ice cream maker.

Per cup: Calories: 165, Protein: 3 gm., Carbohydrates: 30 gm., Fat: 0 gm.

Pineapple Sherbet

Have your ice cream maker ready for this recipe.

Makes 3½ cups

In the blender, mix until smooth:

1 (10.5 oz.) pkg. reduced-fat, firm silken tofu
¼ cup sugar,
    or 2-3 Tbsp. honey
1 Tbsp. lemon juice
½ tsp. vanilla extract
pinch of salt

When this is smooth, add and blend again:

1 (14 oz.) can crushed unsweetened pineapple and
    its juice
¼ tsp. coconut extract (opt.)

Chill the mixture and freeze according to your ice cream maker's directions.

Per serving: Calories: 151, Protein: 2 gm., Carbohydrates: 29 gm., Fat: 0 gm.

Bright Idea . . .

Frozen Bananas

If you see a bargain on ripe bananas, buy the lot and freeze them for fruit shakes, frozen desserts, and baking. Simply peel them, lay them on cookie sheets, and freeze them solid. Store in tightly sealed plastic bags in the freezer.

If you don't have an ice cream maker:

Freeze the blended mixture. Just before serving, break the solidly frozen mixture into chunks, and run it through a heavy duty juicer (according to the manufacturer's directions) or your food processor until just soft. Serve immediately.

Berry and Banana Sherbet
Serve 4-6

The easiest and most delightful frozen dessert.

Place in your food processor, and whiz until smooth:

1 (10 oz.) pkg. frozen berries, lightly sweetened to taste

2 medium frozen bananas, cut into chunks

2 Tbsp. juice, raspberry cassis or other fruit liqueur, or reduced-fat soymilk

Serve immediately.

Per serving: Calories: 62, Protein: 1 gm., Carbohydrates: 14 gm., Fat: 0 gm.

Orange "Julia"
Serves 2

Although this is truly a beverage, it makes a great, light dessert as well.

In a blender, mix until smooth:

¾ cup water

6 Tbsp. orange juice concentrate

¼ cup firm or medium-firm regular tofu

½ tsp. vanilla extract

When the mixture is smooth, add and blend again:

5 ice cubes

Pour into 2 glasses and serve.

Per serving: Calories: 110, Protein: 4 gm., Carbohydrates: 21 gm., Fat: 0 gm.

Mud Pie

Serves 8-10

This frozen dessert is another excellent celebration "cake."

Have ready:

2 cups crumbs from Light and Easy Chocolate Cake or Cupcakes, pg. 148

Mix the crumbs with:

¼ cup maple syrup

Press the mixture into a lightly greased 9" pie plate. Freeze until firm.

Spoon into the frozen crust a fresh batch of:

Coffee Tofu Ice Cream, pg. 171

Smooth the top. Freeze until the ice cream is almost firm, about 1 hour. Drizzle over the top:

1 cup Coffee-Flavored Chocolate Sauce, pg. 177

Swirl it into the ice cream with the back of a knife, creating a marbled effect. Cover with plastic and freeze until firm.

Serve the Mud Pie with *Whipped Soy Cream* pg. 38, which has been flavored with 2 tablespoons coffee liqueur, if desired, instead of vanilla or other flavoring extract.

Per serving: Calories: 308, Protein: 4 gm., Carbohydrates: 62 gm., Fat: 1 gm.

Chocolate Sauce

Makes 1⅓ cups

This easy sauce can be used to flavor drinks or to drizzle over frozen desserts, cakes, and puddings.

In a blender, mix well:

1 cup hot water,
   or reduced-fat soymilk or other non-dairy milk
1 cup granulated sweetener of your choice or
   Sucanat®,
   or ⅔ cup honey
⅔ cup unsweetened cocoa

Pour the mixture into a small, heavy saucepan, and stir over medium-high heat until it comes to a boil. Simmer, stirring, for 1 minute.

Stir in:

2 tsp. vanilla extract

Cool and store in a covered jar in the refrigerator. This will keep for several weeks.

Per 2 Tbsp.: Calories: 96, Protein: 1 gm., Carbohydrates: 21 gm., Fat: 0 gm.

Coffee-Flavored Chocolate Sauce   VARIATION

   Use **coffee** or **coffee substitute** instead of water or soymilk for the liquid.

GLOSSARY

AGAR

Also known as agar-agar or kanten (the Japanese word), this vegetarian gelling agent is made from a seaweed. Like gelatin, it is tasteless and has no calories (but will set at room temperature), so it can be used instead of gelatin in fruit gels and savory aspic. It is widely available in natural food stores in the form of powder, flakes, or bars.

To gel 2 cups of liquid use 1 teaspoon of agar powder, or 2 tablespoons of agar flakes, or about half a bar of kanten. As a comparison, a tablespoon or packet of unflavored, regular gelatin will gel 2 cups of liquid. To use agar flakes instead of agar powder in a recipe, use sixth times as much.

Certain things interfere with the gelling of agar—vinegar and oxalic acid (found in chocolate and spinach), for instance. Fruit acids may soften the gel somewhat—you'll have to experiment with fruit juices to see if you need more than the recommended amount to achieve the degree of firmness that you like. Try using half again as much, especially with citrus, tomato, and pineapple.

BULGUR WHEAT

This quick-cooking wheat product is of ancient origin. Wheat kernels are boiled, dried, and cracked. The resulting bulgur needs only to be cooked for 10 to 15 minutes (1 part bulgur to 2 parts liquid).

CHINESE DRIED MUSHROOM (SHIITAKE)

Shiitake is the Japanese name for Chinese dried mushrooms, or Oriental black mushrooms, as they are sometimes called. They add wonderful flavor to marinades, stews, stir-fries, gravies, sauces, and soups, Store the mushrooms in a cool dry place. To rehydrate them, soak them in boiling water to cover for about 30 minutes, then drain and discard the stems. Use the soaking water in cooking.

CORNSTARCH

Many natural foods cookbooks call for the use of arrowroot powder instead of cornstarch, implying that it is somehow nutritionally superior to cornstarch—it's not. Both are highly refined and not particularly nutritious—arrowroot is much more expensive than cornstarch, however. Since we use only small amounts as thickener, and because cornstarch is more stable, I call for cornstarch.

Actually, cornstarch and arrowroot are not completely interchangeable. Cornstarch needs about 30 seconds of boiling to remove the starchy taste; arrowroot turns clear in very hot liquid without boiling and has no starchy aftertaste.

When arrowroot cools, it becomes rather slimy, so be sure to use cornstarch in recipes that will be served chilled. Arrowroot, on the other hand, is useful for making very glossy, dark hot sauces without fat.

Mix either arrowroot or cornstarch with COLD liquid until smooth before heating or adding to hot food.

EGG REPLACER

Most of the time, eggs can be eliminated or replaced by tofu, soymilk, or cornstarch, but sometimes a commercial egg replacer works best. I use EnerG Egg Replacer, which comes in powdered form and is made from potato and tapioca starches, calcium, citric acid, and carbohydrate gum. Half a tablespoon beaten with 2 tablespoons of water replaces one egg in most baking recipes. Recipes on the box give directions for replacing egg yolks, beaten egg whites, etc.

GARLIC GRANULES

You may wonder why I call for garlic granules instead of garlic powder, when I don't use fresh garlic. This is because garlic granules are made of ground, dried garlic, and garlic power often has starch added, so it is not of the same quality. Garlic granules are available in most supermarkets and in the bulk spice department of natural foods stores.

INSTANT GLUTEN POWDER

Instant gluten powder (also known as vital wheat gluten, "Do-Pep," or pure gluten flour) is available in most natural food stores. The powder is made from gluten, the protein in wheat. Small amounts can be added to breads to improve it for bread-baking, or it can be mixed with cold liquid to make meat substitutes (see pgs. 29-30). The raw gluten is cooked in a flavored broth and is then known by the Japanese name *seitan*.

Do not confuse instant gluten powder with something called "gluten flour." This product is refined wheat flour with gluten powder added. Make sure that it is vital wheat gluten that you are buying.

SOY LECITHIN

Liquid soy lecithin is not strictly a fat—it is a "phospholipid." It is used in the food industry as an emulsifier. I use it only for greasing pans (see *Non-Stick Cooking Blend*, pg. 48), since 1 tablespoon contains almost 14 grams of usable fat (about the same as any oil). Available in natural food stores.

LIQUID SMOKE

This is a useful flavoring to replace the smoky taste of ham, bacon, etc., especially in bean dishes. New studies show that it does not contain carcinogenic impurities, as once thought.

Look for brands that are simply water and natural hickory smoke. Others also contain vinegar, brown sugar, and caramel coloring, but you have to use more to obtain the right results. Add just a few shakes to your dish and taste to see if it is strong enough—you don't need much. It's available in most supermarkets, usually near the barbecue sauces.

MISO

Miso is a Japanese fermented soybean and grain (usually rice or barley) paste which is used as a soup base and a flavoring. It is salty but highly nutritious and valued for its digestive qualities. Unpasteurized miso contains beneficial bacteria similar to that in yogurt, so avoid heating it to the boiling point. If your natural foods store has a selection of misos, try them out to see which you like— there can be a number of varieties: dark, light sweet, mellow, etc. When I call for miso, I'm referring to light brown rice or barley miso.

NUTRITIONAL YEAST

Nutritional yeast is NOT the same thing as brewer's yeast or baking yeast. Nutritional yeast flakes have a cheesy taste and, when mixed with soy sauce or spices, also a rather "chickeny" taste, so they are best used in savory dishes. I also use it in some baking to replace the rich taste of egg yolk.

Yeast is a concentrated source of protein, B-vitamins (some brands have vitamin B-12 added), and minerals, contains no fat and few calories, so it is an important seasoning in vegan cooking. You might like to keep some on your table, like salt, for sprinkling on foods (delicious on popcorn!). You'll find it in natural foods stores.

PASTA

Most fresh pastas are made with eggs, so the pasta recipes in this book call for dried pasta. (You may be able to find fresh pasta made with tofu in some stores). Buy only pasta made from 100% durum wheat flour, not just "wheat flour," "semolina flour," etc.. Durum wheat is high in protein and therefore make a strong, springy pasta. If you can afford it, look for pasta made with organic whole 100% durum wheat flour. Whole durum wheat pasta is light colored, not dark brown, so it is not objectionably "wheaty."

If you are allergic to wheat, there are all kinds of new non-wheat pastas on the market—buckwheat, soy, rice, corn, kamut, spelt, Jerusalem artichoke, mung bean, etc. Try them out to see which you like and be careful not to overcook them.

Always cook pasta in PLENTY of boiling, salted water just until it is "al dente," or still slightly chewy in the middle.

RICE

Whenever possible, use brown rice. It takes longer to cook (unless you use the expensive, new "instant" brown rice), but it is superior to white rice in terms of fiber and nutrients. Brown rice takes about 45 minutes to cook. If you put the rice on before you start the rest of the meal, it'll be done by the time most things are cooked.

Long grain brown rice cooks up in fluffy separate grains; short grain is stickier. There are some delicious varieties of brown rice besides these—brown basmati, Calmati or Texmati, which are very long-grained and aromatic, and wehani, a rust-colored, long grain brown rice with a popcorn aroma and the appearance of wild rice. It's good mixed with regular, long grain brown.

If you prefer white rice, use either white basmati, which is not only delicious, but is not polished, or converted (parboiled) rice, which is steamed before hulling, so that some of the nutrients from the bran are forced into the kernel. Under no circumstances use instant white rice.

To avoid mushy rice, use 1 part rice to 1½ parts water. The Spanish sauté their rice in a little hot oil before adding the liquid—I do this in a dry pan, which also results in dry separate grains. Another way to ensure non-sticky rice is to add it very slowly to boiling water. More sticky, Oriental-style rice is started in cold water.

Both brown and white rice should be brought to a boil, then covered, turned to low heat and simmered until done without lifting the lid or stirring. The lid should fit tightly, and the pot should have a heavy bottom. White rice cooks in 15-20 minutes, brown in 45 minutes. Both improve from standing off the heat with the lid on for 10 minutes.

Rice also comes out nice and fluffy when baked in a 350°-400°F oven. Start it on top of the stove, as instructed above, letting it come to a boil in an oven-proof pot. Then cover and bake for the same amount of time.

You can cook rice in broth, add onion, garlic, herbs, etc. Brown rice should not be cooked with very acid foods such as tomato, which harden the bran layer and make cooking take much longer. Add tomato after the rice has cooked, or use white rice.

For quick-cooking brown rice, soak the brown rice in its cooking water for at least 4 hours (before you go to work, for instance). After soaking, it will cook in 20 minutes!

SOY BACON BITS

This condiment is widely available in grocery stores. It's made with soy flour, soy protein, and artificial and natural flavorings. It does have a bit of oil in it, but, since it is used in small amounts, it will add negligible amounts to your food.

SOY MILK POWDER

Soy milk powder is excellent for adding a little extra protein to baked goods. Do not confuse it with soy flour, which hasn't undergone the same amount of cooking that soy powder has. You can find inexpensive brands in bulk in natural foods stores or more expensive varieties that are suitable for mixing up as beverages, as well as for baking.

SOY SAUCE (SHOYU, TAMARI)

Do not purchase cheap soy sauce that contains hydrolized vegetable protein and caramel coloring. Most supermarkets carry excellent, inexpensive brands of naturally fermented Chinese and Japanese soy sauce. The label should state that it contains only soy beans, salt, water and sometimes wheat. Some manufacturers make "lite" varieties that contain less salt.

Shoyu is the Japanese name for soy sauce. Many brands of soy sauce sold by natural foods manufacturers are labelled "tamari." This is usually a misnomer, because tamari is traditionally a dark, liquid by-product of the miso making process. It is delicious, but not generally available. When a recipe calls for tamari, you can use a good soy sauce.

You'll notice that I use soy sauce in many non-Oriental recipes. It has a meaty, rich flavor that adds body to many recipes. If you have a problem with yeast sensitivities in fermented foods, you can also use liquid aminos for this purpose.

TOFU (BEAN CURD, SOYBEAN CURD)

Tofu comes in many forms—regular (medium-firm, firm, or extra-firm [or pressed]), soft, silken (soft, firm, or extra-firm), marinated, frozen, freeze-dried, and fried. The varieties most often called for in this book are reduced-fat, firm or medium-firm regular, and reduced-fat (or "lite"), firm or extra-firm silken. The regular styles are available in bulk or in vacuum-packaged plastic tubs in many supermarket produce departments and most natural foods stores (the vacuum packs need to be refrigerated and have a "best before" date stamped on them). Soft, firm, and extra-firm silken tofu comes in tetra packs weighing 10.5 oz. and does not need refrigerating until opening. The packs can be stored for about a year, making them great emergency and camping food. Silken tofu has a very creamy, smooth quality with little soy taste, making it excellent for blended dairy substitutes, but it is more expensive than the regular type.

Fresh bulk tofu, or any packaged tofu that has been opened must be kept covered with water in the refrigerator, and the water must be changed daily. It will last a week or two this way. After that time it's best to freeze it in plastic bags (tub tofu can be frozen right in the package).

Frozen tofu becomes spongy and firm. Sliced or crumbled, it soaks up marinades easily and has a pleasant, chewy, meat-like texture. Freeze regular medium-firm, firm, or extra-firm tofu for at least 48 hours. Thaw at room temperature for several hours, or thaw it quickly by immersing in boiling water, changing the water several times until it is thawed through. If the tofu is to be crumbled, squeeze the water out with your hands. Wrap slices of defrosted frozen tofu in layers of clean kitchen toweling, and weight down with a heavy plate for about half an hour.

YEAST EXTRACT

This dark, salty paste with a "beefy" flavor is popular as a spread in England and Australia, but more often used as a broth base in North America. Since it is made from nutritional yeast, it is rich in nutrients. I find the flavor very strong and only use it sparingly in stews and other dishes that need a beefy flavor—I usually mix it with soy sauce. You can find it in the soup or spice section of some supermarkets, natural foods, or specialty foods stores under various brand names, such as Marmite, Vegemite, Vegex, Sovex, and Savorex.

About the nutritional analyses . . .

Calculations for the nutritional analyses in this book are based on the average number of servings listed with the recipes and the avaerage amount of an ingredient, if a range is called for. Calculations are rounded up to the nearest gram. If two options for an ingredient are listed, the first one is used. Not included are optional ingredients, serving suggestions, or fat used for frying, unless the amount of fat is specified in the recipe.

BIBLIOGRAPHY

For in-depth information about low-fat, vegetarian diets and nutrition, and vegetarian diets for children:

Akers, Keith, *Vegetarian Sourcebook*, G. P. Putnam's Sons, N.Y., 1983.

Barnard, Neal, M.D., *Food for Life: How the New Four Food Groups Can Save Your Life*, Harmony Books, N.Y., 1993.

Elliot, Rose, *Vegetarian Mother and Baby Book*, Pantheon Books, N.Y., 1986.

Klaper, Michael, M.D., *Vegan Nutrition Pure and Simple* and *Pregnancy, Children and the Vegan Diet*, Gentle World, 1987. *

Ornish, Dean, M.D., *Eat More, Weigh Less*, HarperCollins, N.Y., 1993, also *Dr. Dean Ornish's Program for Reversing Heart Disease*, Random House, N.Y., 1990

Robbins, John, *Diet for a New America*, Stillpoint, Walpole, N.H., 1987.* (This is a "must read")

*These can be ordered from EarthSave, 706 Frederick St., Santa Cruz, CA 95062.

These publications often provide locations of manufacturers for products not sold in your area:

Vegetarian Gourmet (4 times a year), 2 Public Ave., Montrose. PA, 18801-1220.

Vegetarian Journal (6 times a year), Vegetarian Resource Group, P. O. Box 1463, Baltimore, MD., 21203. (Good articles by vegetarian nutritionists.)

Veggie Life (6 times a year), P. O. Box 55159, Boulder, CO, 80322-7159. (Especially for vegetarians who grow food organically.)

Vegetarian Times (monthly), P.O. Box 570, Oak Park, IL 60303

If you cannot get textured vegetable protein granules, flakes, and chunks, instant gluten powder, and nutritional yeast from stores in your area, you can obtain these products through the mail from:

The Mail Order Catalog
P.O. Box 180
Summertown, TN 38483

or call:
1-800-695-2241

Bean Cooking Times

Use 3 cups of water for each cup of dried beans

Bean	Soaked, open-kettle	No soak and pressure cook	Soak and pressure cook	Yield per 2 cups dry
Aduki	30 min.	15 min.	5-10 min.	6⅔
Anasazi	60 min.	25 min.	15 min.	5
Black	90 min.	30-35 min.	20 min.	5
Black-eyed peas	25 min.	10 min.	5-8 min.	4¾
Chick-pea (garbanzo)	4½ hrs.	35 min.	25 min.	5
Great Northern	90 min.	25 min.	20 min.	5
Kidney	35-40 min.	30 min.	15-20 min.	4½
Lentil, brown*	20-25 min.	**	**	5
Lentil, red *	15-20 min.	**	**	3⅓
Lima, baby	30 min.	10-15 min.	8 min.	4
Navy	35-40 min.	25 min.	15 min.	5
Pinto	90 min.	35-40 min.	20-25 min.	5
Soybeans	**	60 min.	45 min.	4
Split Peas *	75-90 min.	7 min.	**	4

*It is not necessary to presoak lentils and split peas

**Do not use this method for this variety of beans.

Adapted from *Fabulous Beans* by Barbara Bloomfield, Book Publishing Company

Grain Cooking Times

Grain (1 Cup)	Cups Liquid	Salt (optional)	Cooking Times	Yield in Cups
Amaranth	2½	½ tsp. **	20-25 minutes	2
Barley (pot)	3	½ tsp.	55 minutes ***	3½
Buckwheat	2	½ tsp.	10-12 minutes ***	2
Bulgar Wheat	2	½ tsp.	20 minutes ***	3
Couscous	2	½ tsp.	1 minute ***	3
Kamut	3	½ tsp. **	2 hours ***	2¾
Millet	2-3 *	½ tsp.	20-25 minutes	3½-4
Oat Groats	2¼	½ tsp.	1 hour plus ***	2-2½
Quinoa	2	½ tsp.	15 minutes ***	3-3½
Rye Berries	3	½ tsp.	2½ hours ***	2½
Spelt	3	½ tsp. **	2 hours ***	2¼
Triticale	3	½ tsp. **	1¾ hours ***	2-2½
Wheat Berries	3	½ tsp. **	2 hours ***	2¼

* Toast grains lightly in a dry pan before boiling

** Add salt after cooking

***Plus 10 minutes standing time

Index

A

agar 178
Aioli 36
alcohol 17
Apple Pie Filling 154
artificial sweeteners 18

B

bag lunch ideas 65
Baked Beans, Eastern 104
Baked Pâté 58
Baked Tofu, Smoky 24
Banana French Toast 69
Bananas, Frozen 174
Basic
    Barbecue Sauce 44
    Bread Pudding 161
    Light and Easy Muffins 76
    Pancakes 68
    Tofu Ice Cream 171
    Vegetable Stock 86
Bean Dip 54
Bean Dip, Layered "Texas" 55
Beans
    Border 129
    New Orleans-Style Red 132
Beefy Seitan Roast 31
beet sugar 145
Berry and Banana Sherbet 175
Best-Ever Tofu Burgers 124
Biscuits, Drop Scones or 74
blackstrap molasses 146
Blender Fruit Shake 61
Blueberry Muffins 77
Border Beans 129
Bread Dough, Yeast 81
Bread Pudding, Basic 161
Bread Squares, Filled 83
Bread Stuffing 134
Breaded "Breast of Tofu" 23
Breads, Filled 83
"Breast of Tofu", Breaded 23
"Breast of Tofu," Oven-Fried 22
Brown Gravy 43
Brown Sugar Pudding Sauce 169
Browned Flour 49

Brownie Pie, Frozen 172
bulgur wheat 178
Burgers, Best-Ever Tofu 124
Butter, Corn 46

C

Caesar Salad 96
caffeine 18
Cajun Potatoes 139
Cake
    Date Pudding 167
    Fruit Pudding 167
    Hot Fudge Pudding 166
    Lemon Pudding 167
    Light & Easy Basic White 147
    Light & Easy Chocolate 148
    Spice 147
calcium 11
calories from fat 8–9
Caramel Cream Pudding 164
Challah 82
"Cheezy" Salad Dressing 101
Chick-pea a la King 128
Chick-pea a la King Casse-
        role 129
Chick-pea Sandwich Filling 63
children and fat in diet 13
Chile Chunks 111
Chile Sin Carne 130
Chinese dried mushrooms, 178
Chocolate
    Cake, Light and Easy 148
    Cornstarch Pudding 163
    Mousse, Tofu 162
    Sauce 177
    Sauce, Coffee-Flavored 177
    Tofu Ice Cream 172
    Tofu Pie 163
    Tofulato, Frozen 162
Chowder, Corn 91
Cinnamon Sticky Buns, 82
Coating Mix, Seasoned 50
Cocoa Frosting, Lean 149
Coconut Custard 165
Coffee Tofu Ice Cream 171
Coffee-Flavored Chocolate
        Sauce 177
Coleslaw Dressing, Easy 99
Cookies, Frypan 160
cooking gluten to make seitan 29
Corn Butter 46

Corn Chowder 91
Corn "Oysters" 143
cornstarch 178–179
"Cottage Cheese," Tofu 35
Cream Cheese, Tofu 33
Cream Cheese-Fruit Icing 151
Cream Cheeze Icing 151
Cream of Tomato Soup 92
Creamy Dill Dressing 100
Creamy Pasta Sauce 125
Crispy Bars 160
Crispy Oven-Fried Potatoes 139
Crumb Crust 159
Custard, Coconut 165
Cutlets, Simmered Seitan 30

D

daily meal plan, basic 12
Date Pudding Cake 167
Devilled Tofu 57
Dill Dip 56
Dip, Bean 54
Dip, Dill 56
Dressing
    "Cheezy" Salad 101
    Creamy Dill 100
    Easy Coleslaw 99
    Honey-Garlic-Mustard 102
    Low-Fat Poppy Seed 102
    Oil-Free Italian 98
    Sweet and Sour 99
Drop Scones or Biscuits 74
Dry-Roasted Chick-peas 47
Dry-Roasted Soybeans
        ("Soynuts") 47
Dumplings, Featherlight 75

E

Eastern Baked Beans 104
Easy Coleslaw Dressing 99
eating out 14–16
egg replacer 179
Egg-Free French Toast 69
Eggless Salad 57
Enchilada Casserole 116

F

Fat-Free
    Cinnamon Sticky Buns 82
    Fried Rice 123
    "Sausage" 27
    Sweet Yeast Bread Dough 81

Featherlight Dumplings   75
"Feta," Tofu   34
Filled Bread Squares   83
Filled Breads   83
Flour Tortillas   80
French Toast, Banana   69
French Toast, Egg-Free   69
French-Dip Sandwiches   32
Fried Rice, Fat-Free   123
"From the Hearth" Soup   88
Frosting, Lean Cocoa   149
Frozen
   Bananas   174
   Brownie Pie   172
   Chocolate Tofulato   162
   Mocha Tofu Ice   173
Fruit
   Kuchen   156
   Shake, Blender   61
   Sherbet   172
   Syrup   157
   "Yogurt"   70
Frypan Cookies or Crispy
   Bars   160
Fudgesicles   162

G

Garlic Butter   46
garlic granules   179
Garlic Slaw   97
Glaze, Orange or Lemon   150
Glaze, White   150
gluten   29, 179-80
Golden Macaroni Casserole   115
Golden Sauce   41
Golden Vegetable Noodle
   Soup   89
Gomasio, Soy Cheesey   37
Grain and Noodle Pilaf   141
Granola, No-Oil   73
Gravy, Brown   43
Gravy, Yeast   42
"Ground Pork," Fat-Free   28
"Ground Poultry," Fat-Free   28
Guacamole, Low-Fat   60
Gyro, Vegetarian   63

H

Hamburger Rolls, Savory   82
Hash Browns, Oven   138
Hash Browns, Waffle Iron   137

Hero or Gyro, Vegetarian   63
Hollandaise Sauce, Mock   45
"Hollandaise," Tofu   36
honey   146
Honey-Garlic-Mustard Dress-
   ing   102
Hoppin' John   131
Hot Fudge Pudding Cake   166

I

Ice Cream
   Basic Tofu   171
   Chocolate Tofu   172
   Coffee Tofu   171
   Maple Tofu   171
Icing, Cream Cheese-Fruit   151
Icing, Cream Cheeze   151
instant gluten powder   29, 179-80
iron   11

K

Kuchen, Fruit   156

L

Lasagne   108
Layered "Texas" Bean Dip   55
Lean Cocoa Frosting   149
Lemon Glaze   150
Lemon Pudding Cake   167
Lemon Pudding Sauce   169
Light and Easy Chocolate
   Cake   148
Light and Easy Basic White
   Cake   147
Light and Easy Corn Muffins   79
liquid smoke   180
Low-Fat
   American Potato Salad   95
   Guacamole   60
   Poppy Seed Dressing   102

M

Macaroni Casserole, Golden   115
maple syrup   146
Maple Tofu Ice Cream   171
Marinade, Roasting or Grill-
   ing   140
Marinara Sauce, Quick   121
Marinated Tofu Cubes   24
Marmite   184
Mashed Potatoes   136
Mayonnaise, Tofu   36

Milk, Plain Rice   40
Milk, Tofu   39
miso   180
Mocha Tofu Ice, Frozen   173
Mock Hollandaise Sauce   45
molasses, blackstrap   146
Mousse, Tofu Chocolate   162
Mud Pie   176
Muffins
   Basic Light and Easy   76
   Blueberry   77
   Bran   78
   Light and Easy Corn   79
   Orange-Cranberry   77

N

Nachos   55
New Orleans-Style Red
   Beans   132
No-Oil Granola   73
Non-stick Cooking Blend   48
nutritional yeast   180–181

O

oat flour   19
Oil Substitute for Salad Dress-
   ing   98
Oil-Free Italian Dressing   98
Old-Fashioned Rice Pudding   168
Old-Fashioned Vegetable
   Stew   122
Onion Dip, Tofu   53
Orange
   -Cranberry Muffins   77
   Glaze   150
   "Julia"   175
   Pudding Sauce   170
   Sherbet   172
Oven Hash Browns   138
Oven-Fried "Breast of Tofu"   22
Oven-Fried Onion Potatoes   139

P

Pancakes, Basic   68
pasta   181
Pasta Entreés   125
Pasta Sauce, Creamy   125
Pastry, Yeasted   152
Pâté, Baked   58
Pâté Variations   59
Peach Pie Filling   154

percentage of calories from fat
    8-9
Pie
    Apple Filling   154
    Chocolate Tofu   163
    Fillings   154
    Frozen Brownie   172
    Mud   176
    Peach Filling   154
    Pumpkin   155
    Tamale   114
    Tofu Cheezecake   158
Pilaf, Grain and Noodle   141
Pineapple Sherbet   174
Pineapple Sweet & Sour Stir-
    fry   127
Pita Crisps   52
Pitas, Filled   66
Pizza   118
Plain Rice Milk   40
Pot Pie, Tofu   112
Potato Poppers   138
Potato Salad,   95
Potatoes
    Cajun   139
    Crispy Oven-Fried   139
    Mashed   136
    Oven-Fried Onion   139
    Scalloped   135
    Spicy Mexican   139
Pudding
    Basic Bread   161
    Caramel Cream   164
    Chocolate Cornstarch   163
    Fruit Cake   167
    Hot Fudge Cake   166
    Old-Fashioned Rice   168
Pudding Sauce
    Brown Sugar   169
    Lemon   169
    Orange   170
Pumpkin Pie   155

Q

Quesadillas   62
Quick Marinara Sauce   121

R

Rice and Tofu "Yogurt"   70
Rice Milk, Plain   40
Rice Pudding   168

Rice, Spanish   142
rice   181–182
Roast, Beefy Seitan   31
Roasting or Grilling Mari-
    nade   140

S

"Sausage," Fat-Free Italian   28
Salad, Caesar   96
Salad, Eggless   57
Salad, American Potato   95
salt   17
Sandwich Filling, Chick-pea   63
sandwich ideas   64
Sauce
    Basic Barbecue   44
    Brown Sugar Pudding   169
    Chocolate   177
    Coffee-Flavored Chocolate   177
    Creamy Pasta   125
    Golden   41
    Lemon Pudding   169
    Mock Hollandaise   45
    Orange Pudding   170
    Quick Marinara   121
    Tangy Cream   41
    Tartar   36
"Sausage," Spicy Herb   28
"Sausage," Fat-Free   27
Savory Hamburger Rolls   82
Savory Tofu Dinner Loaf   105
Scalloped Potatoes   135
Scrambled Tofu   72
Seasoned Coating Mix   50
Seasoned Flour   49
Seitan
    Beefy Roast   31
    Cutlets 30
    Gluten Balls   30
    Ground   29
    Oven-Fried Chunks   30
seitan   29, 179
Sesame Meal   47
Shake, Blender Fruit   61
Shakes, Tofu   61
Sherbet
    Berry and Banana   175
    Fruit   172
    Orange   172
    Pineapple   174
shiitake mushrooms   178

shoyu   183
Slaw, Garlic   97
Smoky Baked Tofu   24
Soft Vegetable Tacos and
    Burritos   126
Soup
    Cream of Tomato   92
    "From the Hearth"   88
    Vegetable Noodle Soup   89
    Split Pea   90
    Thick Onion   87
Sour Cream, Tofu   37
Southern "Fried" Tofu   110
Soy Cheesey Gomasio   37
Soy Cream, Whipped   38
soy
    bacon bits   182
    lecithin   180
    milk powder   182
    products   9–10, 18
    sauce   183
soymilk, homemade low-fat   18
"Soynuts"   47
Spanish Rice   142
Spicy Mexican Potatoes   139
Split Pea Soup,   90
Starch Glaze   82
steam-frying   19
Stir-Fry "Chicken" Slivers   23
Stir-Fry, Pineapple Sweet &
    Sour   127
Stuffing, Bread   134
substituting textured vegetable
    protein for frozen tofu   26
Sucanat®   145
sugar   17, 144–146
Sweet & Sour Stir-fry   127
Sweet and Sour Dressing   99
sweeteners   144–146
"Swiss Steak"   111
Syrup, Fruit   157

T

Tacos and Burritos, Soft   126
Tamale Pie   114
tamari   183
Tangy Cream Sauce   41
Tartar Sauce   36
Tarts, Toast Crust   66
textured vegetable protein   25–26

Thick and Creamy Split Pea
    Soup 90
Thick Onion Soup 87
Toast Crust Tarts 66
Tofu
    "Bacon" 71
    Burgers, Best-Ever 124
    Cheezecake Pie 158
    Chocolate Ice Cream 172
    Chocolate Mousse 162
    Chocolate Pie 163
    Coffee Ice Cream 171
    "Cottage Cheese" 35
    Cream Cheese 33
    Devilled Tofu 57
    Dinner Loaf, Savory 105
    "Feta" 34
    Frozen Mocha Ice 173
    Ice Cream, Basic 171
    "Hollandaise" 36
    Maple Ice Cream 171
    Mayonnaise 36
    Milk 39

Onion Dip 53
Pot Pie 112
Scrambled 72
Shakes 61
Sour Cream 37
Southern "Fried" 110
Vegetable Scrambled 72
"Yogurt" 35
tofu 183–184
Tofulato, Frozen Chocolate 162
Tortilla Chips, Water-Crisped 52
Tortilla Roll-ups 66
Tortillas, Flour 80
turbinado sugar 145–146

V

Vegetable
    Noodle Soup, Golden 89
    Scrambled Tofu 72
    Stew, Old-Fashioned 122
    Stock, Basic 86
    Tacos and Burritos, Soft 126

Vegetarian
    Hero or Gyro 63
    Shepherd's Pie 106
    Worcestershire Sauce 48
vital wheat gluten 29, 179
vitamin B12 11

W

Waffle Iron Hash Browns 137
Water-Crisped Tortilla Chips 52
Whipped Soy Cream 38
White Cake, Basic 147
White Glaze 150
Worcestershire Sauce, 48

Y

Yeast Bread Dough, Sweet 81
yeast extract 184
Yeast Gravy 42
Yeasted Pastry 152
"Yogurt," Fruit 70
"Yogurt," Rice and Tofu 70
"Yogurt," Tofu 35

photo by Brian Grogan

Bryanna Clark Grogan has been a food writer and teacher for over 20 years. Her interest in cooking began before she can even remember and having her first child sparked a lifelong interest in nutrition. She has four children, two stepsons, two foster sons, numerous grandchildren, and a large extended family (a "small" family get-together might number 18 to 20!).

Bryanna contributes frequently to *Vegetarian Times* magazine, is working on several books, and is a part-time librarian. She lives with husband Brian (her faithful recipe tester) and several children on idyllic Denman Island, off the east coast of Vancouver Island in British Columbia.

Ask your store to carry these books, or you may order directly from:

The Book Publishing Company   *Or call: 1-800-695-2241.*
P.O. Box 99   *Please add $2.00 per book*
Summertown, TN 38483   *for shipping*

American Harvest	11.95
Burgers 'n Fries 'n Cinnamon Buns	6.95
Cookin' Healthy with One Foot Out the Door	8.95
Cooking with Gluten and Seitan	7.95
Ecological Cooking: Recipes to Save the Planet	10.95
Fabulous Beans	9.95
From A Traditional Greek Kitchen	9.95
George Bernard Shaw Vegetarian Cookbook	8.95
Healthy Cook's Kitchen Companion	12.95
Instead of Chicken, Instead of Turkey:	9.95
Judy Brown's Guide to Natural Foods Cooking	10.95
Kids Can Cook	9.95
Murrieta Hot Springs Vegetarian Cookbook	9.95
New Farm Vegetarian Cookbook	8.95
Now & Zen Epicure	17.95
Peaceful Cook	8.95
Physician's Slimming Guide, Neal D. Barnard, M..D	5.95
Also by Dr. Barnard:	
Power of Your Plate	11.95
Live Longer, Live Better (90 min. cassette)	9.95
Beyond Animal Experiments (90 min. cassette)	9.95
Shiitake Way	7.95
Shoshoni Cookbook	12.95
Simply Heavenly	19.95
Soups For All Seasons	9.95
The Sprout Garden	8.95
Starting Over: Learning to Cook w/ Natural Foods	10.95
Tempeh Cookbook	10.95
Ten Talents (Vegetarian Cookbook)	18.95
Tofu Cookery	14.95
Tofu Quick & Easy	7.95
TVP Cookbook	6.95
Uncheese Cookbook	11.95
Uprisings: The Whole Grain Bakers' Book	13.95
Vegetarian Cooking for People with Diabetes	10.95